'In proposing a "kairos-based Christol(
Griffiths offers a theologically rooted a]
young people which offers greater deptl
more narrowly focused incarnational models. Grounded in both
theology and practice, this book is essential reading for those
wanting to be more Christlike in their ministry.'

The Revd Dr Sally Nash, Director of the Midlands
Centre for Youth Ministry and co-author of *The Faith
of Generation Y, Skills for Collaborative Ministry* and
Tools for Reflective Ministry

'I am grateful to Steve for writing this provocative, scholarly
and practically informed contribution to the field of youth
ministry. Steve reclaims the essence of ministering among young
people through a considered exploration of the life of Christ,
unravelling the misconceptions that can lead to an incomplete
presentation of the gospel message. He challenges us to go
beyond the limitations of relational youth ministry and to
embrace "kairos moments" that flow from the youth minister's
spiritual discipline. This should be essential reading for all youth
ministry students and it provides a timely wake-up call to the
seasoned youth minister.'

Paul Fenton, Principal, Oasis College of
Higher Education, London

'This book takes theological thinking on youth ministry forward
in leaps and bounds. It offers a clear challenge that a Christlike
ministry starts with us becoming Christlike. This book will stretch
your thinking on youth ministry and inspire your practice.'

Dr Nick Shepherd, CEO of the Centre for
Youth Ministry

The Revd Dr Steve Griffiths is Rector of the Linton Team Ministry, Cambridge. He has specialized in youth ministry throughout his ministerial career and was Director of the Centre for Youth Ministry at Ridley Hall, Cambridge, from 2005 to 2009. He writes a regular column, 'Saints and Martyrs', for *Youthwork* magazine. He was Chair of the International Association for the Study of Youth Ministry from 2001 to 2009 and was a founding editor of the *International Journal of Youth and Theology*. He has provided extensive training for youth workers in the UK, USA, Scandanavia, Europe and South Africa, and is a regular speaker at conferences. He is also the author of *God in the Valley: A journey through grief* (BRF, 2003; reissued 2010), *Redeem the Time* (Christian Focus, 2001) and a number of academic and popular articles on youth work. You can visit his blog at <http://revdrsteve.posterous.com> and see his tweets @stmaryslinton

Learning from the life of **Christ**

models for YOUTH ministry

STEVE GRIFFITHS

First published in Great Britain in 2013

Society for Promoting Christian Knowledge
36 Causton Street
London SW1P 4ST
www.spckpublishing.co.uk

Copyright © Steve Griffiths 2013

Scripture quotations from the Old Testament are the author's own translation from the
Septuagint, using Brenton's version (Peabody, MA: Hendrickson, 14th printing, May
2011). Quotations from the New Testament are the author's own translation from
the Greek, using the UBS version edited by Kurt Aland *et al.*
(Stuttgart, Germany: United Bible Society, 3rd edn, 1983).

British Library Cataloguing-in-Publication Data
A catalogue record for this book is available from the British Library

ISBN 978–0–281–07051–0
eBook ISBN 978–0–281–07052–7

Typeset by Graphicraft Limited, Hong Kong
First printed in Great Britain by Ashford Colour Press
Subsequently digitally printed in Great Britain

eBook by Graphicraft Limited, Hong Kong

Produced on paper from sustainable forests

This work is dedicated to the students at the Centre for Youth Ministry, Cambridge – past and present – who have graciously allowed me to test out the ideas contained in this book on them over the past few years!

Special thanks, as ever, go to Jo, Scott, Lee and Rebekah

Contents

Contents

Acknowledgements

This book is the product of more than a decade of thinking, writing, teaching and speaking. Unlike most of my other research projects – which are generally crafted in the solitude of my study with only dusty books for companionship – this book has grown out of lectures, seminars and many conversations in which I have participated in the United Kingdom, South Africa, India, the United States, Central Europe and Norway. Literally dozens of youth ministry practitioners and academics helped me to develop my ideas in this first stage. I am grateful to them all for being willing to share their own experiences with me, for the encouragements they gave me and also for pointing out the flaws in my argument.

There has been an evolution in my thinking on this topic. After presenting my ideas in lectures and seminars I published a small book, *A Christlike Ministry* (Haverhill, Essex: YTC Press, 2008), that contained the bare bones of my thesis. Since then, I have continued to refine and apply, to listen and re-consider. I am immensely grateful to all those who have helped me through the second stage of this process.

For support in the first stage, I am grateful especially to the Revd Dr Bob Mayo and Professor Malan Nel for being useful sounding boards. In the second stage, I am grateful to Martin Saunders for giving me a wider platform for my ideas at the 2011 Youthwork Summit. That occasion resulted in very helpful feedback.

I am grateful to Tracey Messenger at SPCK for her patience and wise guidance in helping me think through some of the claims in this book in more depth.

Most especially, I would like to acknowledge the input of my wife, ministry partner and best friend, Jo, who has always been willing to go beyond the call of duty in listening to me long after most people's eyes have glazed over out of sheer boredom!

Introduction

A brief encounter

I was 12, maybe 13 at the time. At that embarrassingly pubescent age, the thought of going to a party with parents was not my idea of fun. But other than the customary complaining that is part of the ritual of conversation with one's elders at that age, I did not complain too much. Despite my necessary protestations, the neighbour hosting the party was actually of considerable interest to me. He had, in his time, been a roadie for a number of my favourite bands, including Pink Floyd and the Rolling Stones. As a novice guitarist, with ambitions way beyond my talent, I was intrigued by the stories he told of life with the rich and famous. Perhaps his party wouldn't be too bad. The music would be good, at least.

Within minutes of arriving, the host introduced me to an Oriental man. 'You should talk to Phil,' he said enthusiastically. 'He's a cracking bass guitarist and session musician. He's played with Ronnie Wood and Rod Stewart.' The fact that I was a fan of neither Ronnie Wood nor Rod Stewart was no barrier to my delight. Here was a real musician! I was in awe of the demi-god in whose presence I now stood.

I don't remember our conversation. But I do remember the fact that he sat politely with me on the stairs for four hours as I pounded his ears and saturated his brain with questions. I do remember the extraordinary patience of a man who was forced to regale an acne-covered schoolboy with stories of his even more extraordinary career. I do remember the fact that his eye contact never wavered and that he almost looked interested as I enthusiastically took him through the extent of my repertoire after only six months of playing. I do remember that he gave me a plectrum. He said it was Ronnie Wood's. I've still got it.

It may or may not have once belonged to someone famous. Probably didn't. But that's not the point, is it?

What I remember from that encounter is a man who was willing to give time, to sacrifice his enjoyment of a good party, for a young person. Me.

I'm sure that, 30 years later, he doesn't even remember me. But I remember him. If you're reading this book Phil, thanks for a great night!

Seeing what's really there

This book has been written out of a deep sense of frustration, for two reasons.

First, for a number of years, I have had a sense of frustration about the way in which Christology has provided a model for ministry. There is nothing wrong with using Christology in this way – of course not! If I felt it an inappropriate model, I would not have added yet another book to the already burgeoning shelves containing such works. My frustration has come about because I believe that previous books written, while good in as far as they have gone, have been too limited in scope. Much has been written in recent years about what has become known as incarnational ministry or relational ministry – especially in the world of youth ministry. In order to theologize about the concept, Christology has been used as the basis for approach. This is right and proper. However, in so doing, Christology has been limited to an analysis of incarnation only.

Put simply – or caricatured – the approach has been this: the Word became flesh, therefore our calling in youth ministry is to 'flesh the Word' among young people. Out of this has grown an approach to ministry that has been profoundly relational – but little more than that. Youth workers are encouraged to spend time with young people, as Jesus spent time with people; to 'hang out' with youth as Jesus hung out with his disciples.

As a result, the kerygmatic imperative has become replaced with the methodology of 'earning the right' to share the gospel after a period of time has passed. By this I mean that youth workers are often reluctant, for whatever reason, to be proactive in speaking the gospel openly to unbelieving young people at an early stage of encounter. Instead, it has become a more common practice to wait until relationships are well established and secure before such conversations begin. Such an approach places the power of decision entirely in the hands of young people; youth workers must wait until they are given permission to present the gospel. If this is the methodology of practice, the youth worker may 'see the need' but be impotent in addressing the need until the young person personally initiates the process of spiritual interaction.

As I listen to the experiences that youth workers describe, and hear the deep-rooted frustration they often feel about not having the opportunities they crave to share the gospel, I cannot get rid of the nagging feeling that there must be something more to a christological foundation for ministry. In fact, I sometimes feel that the notion of 'relational youth ministry' is often used as an excuse for theological and ministerial laziness! Let me be clear at this point. I am not for one moment suggesting that the majority of youth workers are inherently lazy. What I am suggesting is that those of us involved in training and mentoring youth workers have often been guilty of providing lazy theological frameworks for ministry. Quite simply, we have not given youth workers an adequate christological foundation for their ministries. If they have not been told, how can they practise differently? As I will argue in this book, I do not believe the christological approach so often practised by youth ministers to be a true reflection of the approach that Jesus took.

There is, in a sense, a dual calling arising out of this book. First, those of us actively involved in training and mentoring youth workers need to repent of our own theological laziness and be prepared to seek a deeper understanding of Christ to teach and model to those we nurture. Second, youth workers must be prepared to grapple with the impact on their own practice that a more rounded christological framework may have for them. This will inevitably involve a review of what is currently done as well as a passion to develop new practices.

Which brings me to the second point of frustration that I have felt over the years. This relates to my own experience in youth ministry. Relational youth ministry presupposes that the youth worker has a considerable period of time to 'come alongside' a young person or group of young people. The reality is, however, that many of us do not have the luxury of such extended periods of time with young people. It is certainly the case in the United Kingdom and, I suspect, elsewhere in the world too, that youth workers will only stay in a particular post for about three years before moving on elsewhere. The first few months are spent getting a feel for the ministerial situation while the energy of the final year is often devoted to looking for another post and then putting structures in place that will ensure the longevity of the project after departure. That being the case, only 18 months to two years may be spent focusing exclusively on the young people. That is not a long time to build meaningful relationships. Furthermore, the transient nature of society is such that young people we work with may move on before we do. Perhaps they will go to university in another town. Perhaps their parents will divorce and they must move away. Perhaps one of their parents will have a job relocation that demands a house move. Perhaps they will find a new friendship group and just drift away. Whatever the reason, we often lose touch with young people before having had a chance to bond with them to an extent where we have 'earned the right' to present the gospel. This is the reality for many of us working alongside young people. That being the case, it seems to me that the traditional model of relational youth ministry is fast becoming moribund.

There are only two possible conclusions that we can reach. Either relational ministry (or incarnational ministry) is a concept that has had its day and must be replaced with something more contemporary or else we need to find a different way to interpret the concept. It is the latter conclusion that I am endorsing in this work. I do not believe that incarnational ministry has had its day. I do believe, however, that we need a new understanding of what incarnational ministry actually is. It is this idea that I shall be outlining in the work that follows. What is more, I propose that the model I am outlining is more profoundly christological than the traditional exposition, for one good reason; namely, that Jesus of Nazareth did not model an incarnational ministry in the way that has often been described.

Contrary to popular opinion, the truth is that Jesus did not 'hang out' with people. Jesus did not wait to 'earn the right' before embarking on the kerygmatic imperative. Indeed, the very opposite is true. His earthly ministry lasted only two or three years. In that time, he constantly wandered the countryside, towns and cities of Israel, never staying in one place long enough to build relationships with those he met. It may not be an exaggeration to state that, in reality, Jesus had a 'hit and run' ministry. He went into a particular region, taught, healed the sick and then, within a matter of hours or days, moved on elsewhere. That was the pattern of his ministry.

'Well,' you may argue, 'that might be so. But he spent a long time building relationships with his disciples, didn't he?' Again, I would argue that he did not. To be sure, he lived with the disciples 24/7 and went through some intensely traumatic times with them. Nevertheless, he did not have a long time with them. While Jesus' public ministry lasted two or three years, that does not equate to two or three years with his disciples. We must subtract the time he spent in the wilderness after his baptism. We do not know what the time-gap was between Mark 1.15 (when Jesus announced the nearness of the kingdom of God) and Mark 1.16 (when Jesus called Simon, Andrew, James and John). A further, considerable period of time passed before the last eight disciples were appointed; Jesus had time to spend in Capernaum, complete a preaching tour, return to Capernaum, undertake healings, call Levi, and teach in the synagogue before the final selection happened in Mark 3.13–19. In addition to this, the disciples were then sent out in pairs to undertake mission without Jesus (Mark 6.7–13) as well as their probable participation in the broader mission activity of the 70 sent out by Jesus (Luke 10.1–12). It is clearly a myth to believe that Jesus spent three, intensive, years with his disciples. He did not. Simon, Andrew, James and John had more time with him than the remaining eight named disciples (Levi had been called in Mark 2.14 but appears to have remained in the circle of people who followed Jesus but were not called 'disciples'). It is difficult to make any rational claim for Jesus 'hanging out' with his disciples for very long at all. Indeed, it seems likely that Jesus spent little more than a year with his inner group of followers.

The truth is that Jesus did not model a relational ministry after the manner in which that has often been interpreted to us. That is not to say that Jesus was not relational or that he did not value relationships: far from it. However, it is too simplistic to suggest that we must spend years and years with a group of young people before we have 'earned the right' to speak the gospel to them as if that is staying true to the example of Jesus.

'Time' and youth ministry

Far from posing a difficulty for the development of youth ministry, this re-framing of Christology actually liberates us to become more effective. This becomes possible when we consider the notion of 'time' in relation to ministry. This is a concept that will underpin what follows in each chapter of this book, so it is worth taking a little detour at this stage to consider two different New Testament concepts of 'time', expressed through the Greek words *chronos* and *kairos*.

Chronos (χρόνος) is a Greek word used in the New Testament to speak of a measurable period of time (for example, Monday through to Wednesday or 11.00 in the morning through to 3.00 in the afternoon). There are dozens of reference to *chronos*-time in the New Testament, but the following examples will illustrate three key ways in which the biblical writers use the word.

First, *chronos* can speak of a definite period of extended time. In Luke 8.27, for example, we are told that the Gerasene demoniac had worn no clothes 'for a long time'. Likewise in John 7.33, Jesus told the disciples that he would be with them 'a little time'. What is expressed in these passages is a measurable period, a defined period of time. It is not at all unusual in the New Testament for the exact length of *chronos* to remain undisclosed, however. There is often a sense that, even though *chronos* is a definite period, the importance of that period is contained in the events that fill it rather than the measure of time itself.

Second, *chronos* can refer to a specific moment in measured time. In his speech to the Council recorded in Acts 7, Stephen recounts the history of God's people. In verse 17 he says, 'And as the time of the promise drew near, which God swore to Abraham'. Stephen uses the word *chronos* to speak of a specific moment when the promise would be fulfilled; the act of God breaking into history at a definite and measurable moment in time.

Third, *chronos* can refer to a long period of time composed of several shorter ones. In Titus 1.2, Paul refers to 'the hope of life eternal which God, who cannot lie, promised before time eternal'. It seems that Paul is subdividing the history of the world, or more specifically, the history of the people of God, into various 'ages' but contextualizing the place of each of these within a broader, holistic, movement of God.

So from the biblical use of the word, we might argue that *chronos* is a definite period of extended time, often subdivided into shorter periods of engagement that may contain within them key encounters. That being the case, it seems clear to me that relational youth ministry, as traditionally formulated, is wholly dependent on the interpretation of time as *chronos*. The idea is that ministry becomes effective as more and more *chronos*-time is spent building relationships. We devote *chronos*-time to hanging out with young people, earning the right to eventually share the gospel with them. The idea underpinning this form of ministry is that the more *chronos*-time we devote to young people, the more likely it is that a key encounter will happen. As a result, we become addicted to the development of programmes that will extend *chronos*-encounter with young people. We are constantly putting on events, running groups, filling our diaries with 'stuff' in the hope that we may be able to snatch a holy encounter in the midst of the busyness.

But as we noted above, the difficulty with this methodology is that few of us actually have enough *chronos*-time to be effective. Perhaps our ministry ends as we move on to pastures new or the circumstances of the young people we work with change and they move on. Or perhaps there simply are not enough hours in the day to create the spaces for encounter that we need to be effective. Therefore, a ministry that is built primarily on *chronos*-time results in overwhelming frustration at best and a deep-seated sense of guilt at worst as we reflect on opportunities squandered or an inadequate period of time to make a real difference. It seems to me that this purpose-driven approach is the chief cause of ministerial burnout among Christian youth workers. Surely, there must be a better way.

The better way is found in considering the alternative notion of 'time' in the New Testament; that of *kairos*-time. We must be clear that the notion of *kairos* (καιρός) does not stand in direct juxtaposition to *chronos* in as much as there is a certain amount of overlap between the two; there are instances in Scripture where perhaps either word would have conveyed the meaning of the text. However, there is an important semantic sense in which the word *kairos* does not speak of measuring time as duration so much as quality. Let us consider three key examples of the use of *kairos* in this regard.

First, *kairos* can speak of the quality that fills a moment or period of *chronos*-time. In 2 Corinthians 6.2, Paul uses the word *kairos* when he says, 'Behold, now the acceptable time; behold, now the day of salvation'. The day itself is a *chronos* measurement, but Paul uses the word *kairos* to express the fact that this *chronos*-moment is actually defined by the *kairos*-quality of salvation.

Second, the word *kairos* is often used to define the purpose or character of a specified period of time or an event. In Galatians 4.10, Paul notes that his readers are observing 'days, and months, and seasons, and years'. Likewise, in Matthew 13.30, Jesus refers to the 'time of the harvest'. In both these examples, it is the purpose of the moment that is important, rather than just the moment itself.

Third, and crucially, *kairos* is the key word used to describe eschatological purpose. In Chapter 6, we will consider this in some detail. Suffice to say at this stage that the biblical writers infuse *chronos*-time with eschatological meaning by reference to the *kairos*-quality contained within. The end times are referred to as *kairos* in a number of places (for example, Mark 13.33; 1 Timothy 4.1). Crucially, in Acts 1.7, Jesus himself juxtaposes *chronos* with *kairos*, noting that both must be fulfilled before the final consummation: 'It is not yours to know times (*chronos*) or seasons (*kairos*) which the Father set by his own authority'.

If we interpret *kairos* as the quality or meaning that inhabits *chronos*, it becomes clear that we experience *kairos*-moments when we enjoy a moment of meaning with another individual, or creation, or God. The moment of meaning may be fleeting in terms of *chronos*, but it is of eternal value in terms of *kairos* because *kairos*, by definition, is only measurable by eternal value.

The contention of this book is that, in developing relational ministry, Jesus was not so much operating in *chronos*-time as *kairos*-time. This is more than a nuance; it is a factor that is crucial to interpretation if we are to be freed from feelings of frustration and guilt as we seek to become effective in youth ministry.

Too often, relational ministry has been expounded from a christological model that is founded on a *chronos*-approach. If we re-frame that to be founded on a *kairos*-approach, it no longer matters how many years or months or days or hours or even minutes we have to spend with a particular young person or group of young people. Instead, even the briefest encounter with a young person can become a moment of meaning as a *kairos*-event. A single conversation or action has the possibility of being abundant with the Eternal. That is relational ministry as modelled to us by Jesus. He did not have to spend days and weeks in a particular town, earning the right to proclaim the good news. The Gospels are packed with stories of Jesus acting out a *kairos*-ministry; seizing the moment and packing every encounter with a taste of eternity.

Jesus built relationships, not through spending *chronos*-time with individuals but expending energy in seizing *kairos*-moments. Jesus would transform lives by teaching – and then move on. He would restore wholeness through an act of healing – and then move on. He would turn the natural order upside down by raising the dead – and then move on. Jesus' ministry was, first and foremost, a *kairos*-ministry. If we are to develop youth ministry based on Christology, we too are called away from *chronos*-concern towards *kairos*-commitment. It is this truth that most profoundly liberates us to become effective in whatever circumstance we find ourselves.

Building on solid rock

If this is the case, we are further bound to recognize that a successful youth ministry is not dependent on programmes or strategies. Instead, it is fundamentally dependent on a strong personal spirituality. Jesus was only ever able to recognize and seize the *kairos*-moment because he spent so much time in prayer and in the presence of his Father. Jesus spent hours every day in personal spiritual preparation. Then, when he had a relational encounter, he was spiritually aware enough to see straight into the heart of the situation and maximize that moment, filling it with an eternal (eschatological) quality. The same is true for all of us involved in youth ministry. The hard work is not taken up in face-to-face contact with young people. The hard work of youth ministry is taken up in the small, quiet hours of daily prayer and Bible study. Quite simply, we are only ever able to embark effectively on a *kairos*-ministry if we first prepare our hearts in the presence of our Father.

Youth ministry is, first and foremost, a spiritual ministry. It is out of a rich personal spirituality that we are able to form relationships that can make a difference. Those of us who are involved with training youth workers would do well to revisit our curricula to see whether or not we devote enough time and energy to spiritual formation. As crucial as these are to effective and professional standards in ministry, the primary calling of a Christian youth worker is not to understand theories or management-styles or even current legislation. The primary calling of a Christian youth worker is to know the will of the Father and to model his or her ministry on that of Jesus Christ in order to have the ability to truly seize the *kairos*-moments that present themselves. Everything we teach youth workers – the theories, the theology, the good practice, the professional values – must support this primary goal.

The rest of this book is devoted to developing christological models that enable us to understand youth ministry from the perspective of *kairos*, not *chronos*. It is no longer enough to think of the traditional understanding of incarnational ministry as the be-all and end-all of christological approaches. To be sure, it is a part of the approach. But the life and ministry of Jesus gives us many more riches to consider and draw into our own approach with young people.

It is this agenda that *Models for Youth Ministry: Learning from the life of Christ* seeks to address.

Pause for thought

- In what ways is your current youth work practice based on the idea of *chronos* rather than *kairos*?
- What are the pressures you feel as a result of not having enough *chronos*-time to spend with young people?
- What are the expectations of your organization with regard to *chronos*-activity? How might you begin challenging these expectations?
- What support do you need to begin focusing your ministry on *kairos* rather than *chronos*? How might you go about accessing that support?

1

Developing a Christology for ministry

Christology focuses on Jesus Christ. It is Christ-*ology*. The 'ology' part comes from the Greek word *logos* (λόγος), which means 'word'. Therefore, Christology is Christ-words, Christ-talk. Christology is our ideas about who Jesus Christ was and is.

This is a book about the importance of Christology as a model for Christian youth ministry. For those of us involved with nurturing others in the faith, it is vital that we get our Christology right. Why? Because the development of an appropriate Christology is the ultimate challenge which Jesus himself has given to all who want to follow him in a life of discipleship. Perhaps you are familiar with that amazing moment in Mark 8 when Jesus and his disciples are coming near the villages of Caesarea Philippi. What an amazing place that was! Caesarea Philippi, in the olden days, had been a real focus of Ba'al worship. There was also a cavern in the hills where, it was said, the Greek god Pan was born. Right at the top of the hill, there was a temple dedicated to Caesar worship. Quite deliberately, against this background of pluralist religious belief and faith-history, Jesus asks his disciples the ultimate question: 'You? Who do you say I am?' In the midst of this pagan environment, Jesus poses the ultimate question.

'And you? Who do you say that I am?' That is the question Christ asks everyone who encounters him and is encountered *by* him. In today's world, perhaps more than ever before, young people are confronted with many different ways to respond to that question. There are so many different ideas about Jesus. Some of these arise from a re-interpretation or re-contextualization of ancient Christian teaching and tradition, such as feminist theology, liberation theology or gay theology. Others arise out of encounter with other faiths – the Jesus of Islam, the Jesus of Hinduism and so forth. Still others arise out of the array of political interest groups that claim Jesus as a foundation for their ideals; Christian Socialism and some proponents of the Big Society among others. The very nature of our pluralistic, multi-ethnic, multi-cultural, multi-interest society is such that it is possible to make one of any number of responses to the question of who Jesus is. Notwithstanding the importance of these cultural perspectives and the truths contained within them, we want the young people among whom we live and to whom we minister to answer with Peter, 'You are the Christ.' Our desire is to introduce them to the Jesus who is the Christ, the Son of the Living God and for them to find appropriate theological and cultural expressions for this confession of faith.

However, if we want young people to respond to the truth of who Christ is, we must have a well-developed Christology to underpin our own ministry. If our Christology is weak, our theology is weak. Why? Because the words and actions of Christ are the words and actions of God himself. If we misunderstand and misinterpret Christ, we misunderstand and misinterpret God. The contention of this book is that Christian youth ministry must necessarily be founded upon a valid model of Christology. We are called to teach Christ. We are called to model Christ. When we teach young people to pray, we are helping them to build a relationship with God the Father through Jesus Christ. When we disciple them in the ways of holiness, it is a righteousness through union with Christ that is being developed. There are many other examples of Christian doctrine and practice that can only be fully comprehended in the light of Christology; our approaches to baptism, the Eucharist, spiritual gifts, healing, forgiveness and reconciliation to name but a few. Our words, our lifestyle and the practical outworking of our Christian beliefs must be a reflection of Christ to others. Christology is our foundation for ministry.

A scriptural framework for Christology

Whether or not we have consciously considered this issue, we all have a Christology. As we have engaged in Christ-talk through the years, we have developed ideas about who we think Christ is. There are many influences on how we develop our Christology; the ideas of others, media portrayals, fictional and non-fictional books, sermons we have heard preached, artistic interpretations, doctrines taught in non-Christian faiths and so on. However, the primary source for the development of a valid Christology must be the Scriptures. There are three reasons for this.

First, Scripture provides the context for Christology. The event of Jesus Christ cannot be divorced from the story of the people of Israel as recounted in the Old Testament nor the development of the Church as recounted in the New Testament. The life and ministry of Christ – what we might call 'the Christ-event' – is the pivotal point of the biblical witness. That truth is even reflected in the name 'Jesus Christ'. 'Jesus' is derived from the Hebrew *Joshua*, which means 'to save'. 'Christ' is a title from the Greek *christos*, which means 'anointed one, messiah'. The amalgamation of the two is a coming together of the ancient Hebrew tradition of the Old Testament and the Greek influence in the Church of the New Testament. Jesus Christ – by definition – is not only the pivotal event of Scripture but also the defining moment of history. The Old Testament era builds up to Jesus. The New Testament era is founded on Christ. Jesus is historically located within the narrative that includes Abraham, Moses, Saul, David, Peter, Paul, Cornelius, James and John.

The story of Scripture is his context and we cannot fully understand Jesus Christ outside of that. The New Testament writers were at pains to help us locate Christ within the broader story of the people of Israel. That is immediately clear from the genealogy that Matthew provides for us at the beginning of his Gospel (1.1–17) and the way in which many other writers use Old Testament passages as prophecies of Jesus (for example, 1 Peter 2.22). The letter to the Hebrews is dedicated to the exposition of Christ as the fulfilment of God's promises to his people. The complete canon of Scripture is therefore the proper context for Christology. History testifies to the importance of this for Christian youth ministry. Two examples will suffice.

If we do not locate our Christology within the context of the Old Testament, we may be in danger of falling into the heresy known as Marcionism. To cut a long theological story short, Marcion was a second-century theologian who believed that the god of the Old Testament was a different god from the one portrayed in the New Testament. Unable to reconcile images of anger and wrath with the images of love, mercy and forgiveness, Marcion concluded that the Old Testament portrayed a 'lesser god'. His conclusion was to encourage an abandonment of the Old Testament in favour of the teaching of the New. While we may recoil at the accusation of being a Marcionite heretic, I suspect that there is more than a hint of Marcionism in the way many of us use Scripture in ministry. There is a real temptation for us to avoid the 'difficult bits' with young people. Many of us are far happier expounding one of Paul's letters than an obscure part of Leviticus or Kings or Chronicles. We are more comfortable in leading them to passages of love rather than those that recount stories of pillage and genocide. However, if we do avoid the tough passages in the Old Testament, it becomes difficult to develop a balanced Christology that is not afraid of teaching the wrath of God, the power of sin, the need for obedience and the reality of judgement. If we avoid the tough passages in the Old Testament, we are in no position to examine the hard sayings of Christ.

Christology must necessarily find its context within a holistic approach to the Old Testament if we are to challenge young people with the claims of Christ on their lives. I remember Pete in my youth group a few years back. He habitually used inappropriate language about other people in the group, particularly the girls. When I challenged him about this he would say, 'I know it's wrong and I have said "Sorry" to Jesus for it. It's OK, he's forgiven me.' His cavalier approach to this pattern of behaviour frustrated me a great deal and I felt angry towards him. Only slowly did I realize that I was partly at fault because I had never really addressed the idea of God as an angry judge with him or the wider group; I was always talking about grace and mercy and forgiveness and our ability to have a fresh start with God each day. While that aspect of the Christian faith is true, I had presented an unbalanced gospel and so was not in a position to challenge his behaviour. I wanted to draw his attention to Paul's words in Romans 6.15: 'What then? Should we sin because we are not under law but under grace? Certainly not.' But I realized I first had to re-present Christ to him in a more holistic fashion for Paul's words to carry any weight.

In the same way that we cannot divorce the story of Christ from the Old Testament, our Christology cannot be divorced from the New Testament because all that follows the Gospel narratives reveals the truth that God has a plan for universal salvation. God tasked Israel to be 'a light to the nations'. As Christians, we are tasked by God to be 'lights to the world'. Through Jesus Christ, God has a plan of salvation that embraces every race, colour and social grouping on earth. The New Testament is the story of the impact of Christ in action. The New Testament is the story of what happens when people are embraced by Jesus Christ and receive the salvation that he offers. If we divorce Christology from the New Testament, there is no story worth believing. During the first half of the twentieth century, urban youth ministry in London was transformed through the extraordinary efforts of Reginald Kennedy Cox.

17

At the heart of his ministerial success was the need to address the impoverishment of urban young people and fight for justice and improvement of social living conditions. However, he was absolutely convinced that this could only be effective by locating social action firmly within a christologically based practice. In his book *Through the Dock Gates*, he wrote, 'Without religion all that is left are the bare bones of intellectual reform, with none of that divine pity and understanding, running through the whole effort, which makes the impossible become possible, whatever cynics may think to the contrary' (1939: 221).

In short then, the Old Testament helps us have a holistic view of Christ and the New Testament helps us see the impact of Christ. Scripture is necessarily the context for a Christology that can underpin our ministry.

Second, Scripture provides the content of our Christology. Quite simply, what we know about Jesus Christ – the information on which we build our Christology – is found in Scripture. What we believe about Jesus Christ is what we believe about a particular person who lived in a particular place at a particular time. What we believe about Jesus Christ is what we believe about a particular person who did particular things and made particular claims for himself. Christology is not about abstract ideas. It is about a person named Jesus. When we are nurturing others in the faith, we are not teaching them ideas. Rather, we are introducing them to a person: Jesus of Nazareth. It is the unfolding story of Scripture that most effectively ties our faith to the historical event that was – and remains – Jesus Christ.

Furthermore, the scriptural witness that attests to this person Jesus Christ is both accurate and reliable. While each of the Gospel writers focuses on a different perspective about Jesus Christ, there is an essential agreement about him. No Gospel presentation of Christ contradicts any other. There is an inherent reliability attested to concerning his ministry.

Especially in the Gospel narratives, a most remarkable man confronts us: a man with a deep relationship with God; a man seeped in prayer; a man with a profound sense of mission and a real vision for his own ministry; a man who was courageous in challenging the *status quo*; a man of love and compassion; a man of forgiveness; a man who reached out to the outcast, the whores and the hated; a man who loved the vulnerable and the poor; a man who embodied love and justice and mercy and grace; a man who brought healing to those who hurt. The Scriptures portray Jesus as a quite remarkable individual who revealed God to the world. Klaas Runia was right in commenting that, 'All [the New Testament] writers, in one way or another, put Jesus on the side of God' (1995: 19), because the divinity of Christ is not just expressed in the Gospel narratives. The history of the early Church, as recorded in the Acts of the Apostles and the other pastoral and theological writings of the first few centuries, suggests that the biblical portrayal of Jesus is accurate. The manner in which the Church grew, the way in which lives were changed, the courageous witness of the first Christian martyrs, all testify to the fact that everything we have read about Jesus is true. He really is that most remarkable man who is attested to in Scripture and who is the basis of our Christology.

Crucially, however, we recognize that the content of Christology that we want young people to experience is primarily a content of *kairos* rather than *chronos*. That is to say, we do not want young people to merely understand the facts about Jesus, or the timeline of his life on earth. Instead, we are concerned for them to experience afresh the eternal quality of Christ depicted in the life and ministry of the man from Nazareth. Historically, the Church has occasionally gone awry in this pursuit of *kairos*, most notably in the writing of theologians such as Rudolf Bultmann in the twentieth century. In essence, Bultmann discounted the need for any real engagement with the historical person of Jesus of Nazareth, since the power of the gospel is not located in him so much as in *faith* in him. We do not want to go that far! It seems to me that the reality of *kairos* can only be found through *chronos*-activity, not divorced from it. We must teach our young people about the Christ who ministered in and through *chronos*-time, even though the depth of meaning is not located in the *chronos* but in the *kairos*-quality that inhabited each of his *chronos*-encounters. This is important, as we shall discover in Chapter 6 when we consider the theology of hope in relation to youth ministry.

Third, Scripture affirms the continuity of Christology in that there is continuity between the way the New Testament writers portrayed Christ and the manner in which he himself thought about his own mission. This is a vital point to consider because if the biblical writers misunderstood Jesus' mission, there would be a clash of ideals that would cause insurmountable problems for mission and ministry.

Of course, this is a contentious theme in theology. There has been a great deal of debate through the years about the extent to which the earliest followers of Jesus (and then the developing Church) had a different understanding of his mission than the Messiah himself did. Alfred Loisy was a keen proponent of this view in the early twentieth century but we see the continuing influence of this idea most especially in liberation theologies. There is undoubtedly some truth in this perspective, most especially with regard to the way in which the Church has engaged with power in an 'unChristlike' manner. We are indebted to the ministry and prophetic witness of Shane Claiborne for his continuous and uncompromising challenge to the contemporary Church to rediscover the principles and practices of Jesus of Nazareth and redefine Church accordingly. In *Jesus for President: Politics for Ordinary Radicals*, Claiborne writes, 'The history of the church has been largely a history of "believers" refusing to believe in the way of the crucified Nazarene and instead giving in to the very temptations he resisted – power, relevancy, spectacle' (2008: 165). While we accept this historical critique, does that necessarily mean that the historical Jesus has become lost in the mists of time, replaced with a messianic icon, a theological creation moulded and shaped by the development of ideas in time?

One great theologian who worked on this problem was Professor C. F. D. Moule in his book, *The Origin of Christology*. In part, what Moule did was to liken Christology to biology and outline the vital difference between *evolution* and *development*: 'if, in my analogy, "evolution" means the genesis of successive new species by mutations and natural selection along the way, "development", by contrast, will mean something more like the growth, from immaturity to maturity of a single specimen within itself' (1977: 2). Moule then goes on to suggest that, in Scripture, we see a 'developing Christology' not an 'evolving Christology'. That is to say, there is only one Christology in Scripture but, as the years went by and more and more books and letters got written, ideas about who Jesus Christ was and is developed. There was a process of maturing happening in the Scriptures. This explains the difference between, for example, the Christology of Mark's Gospel (written soon after the death of Jesus) and the Christology of John's Gospel (written many years later). Christology *developed* in the period during which the Scriptures were written. What did *not* happen, according to Moule, was an *evolution* of Christology. Evolution implies mutation from one type of being to another. The self-understanding of who Jesus was did not mutate into something different at the hands of Paul and John and the other biblical writers.

There was a *development* but not an *evolution* that demanded a new language as the years went by. Three such examples shall suffice to prove the point. First, Jesus believed that he had a precious relationship with God that could only be expressed in the phrase 'Abba, Father' (Mark 14.36). Hence, the New Testament writers claim him to be 'the Son of God' (for example, Romans 1.3; Hebrews 1.2; 2 Peter 1.17; 1 John 1.3). Second,

Jesus believed himself to be charged with the task of creating a covenant community of disciples and believers (Mark 1.16–20; 3.13–18). Hence, Paul portrays him as head and Lord of the Church (Colossians 1.18). Third, Jesus had an innate awareness that he was God's anointed one for that moment and that task. The New Testament writers allude to the Old Testament messianic prophecies by referring to Jesus as the Son of Man. Many other examples could be given to prove the continuity between what Jesus thought about himself and his own mission and how the New Testament writers portrayed his ministry.

That continuity of thought is vital if we are to create a coherent Christology for the young people we serve and for ourselves. The Christian faith is not based on an idea or an ideology. The Christian faith is not a philosophical principle. The Christian faith is founded on God revealing himself through a particular man at a particular moment in time. As Christians, we are not called to believe an idea. We are called to forge a relationship. So, just like any other relationship we may enter into, it is vital that we develop a reliable understanding of the person of Jesus Christ. Scripture vouchsafes that reliability by providing context, content and continuity for Christology. Without a Christology firmly founded upon the Scriptures, the young people to whom we minister will be like boats tossed around by the waves of life, rudderless and with no anchor to hold them firm.

A cultural framework for Christology

The need for a scriptural Christology is, of course, only half the story. No doctrinal idea can stand in isolation. It must always be in dialogue with the culture in which it is being presented. The question with which we must grapple is this: how do we move from a series of writings about a man who lived 2000 years ago in a backwater location in the Middle East to a Christology that makes sense and empowers people in twenty-first-century Western society? Unfortunately, many

Churches and teachers of the faith have fallen foul of the temptation to forget the 2000 years between Jesus' time and our own. Too often we are presented with a leap of logic that defies time and location: 'The Scriptures teach us XYZ about Jesus, so XYZ is what we should teach to others.' If only it were that simple! The element that is missing from such an approach is one that interprets the christological teaching of Scripture in the light of the culture in which we live and minister. Just as importantly is another missing element; how to interpret the culture in the light of that christological teaching from Scripture.

The truth of the Christian faith throughout history is that there has always been interplay between 'the raw data of faith' and the culture in which that data is expressed. Differences in culture, geography and time mean that the common Christology of Scripture must necessarily be expressed in a plurality of ways. The same faith – the same Christ – explained and explored differently according to the cultural setting of the writer and audience. For example, I have had cause to give serious theological reflection in two radically different youth ministry contexts to the saying of Jesus in Matthew 10.42, 'Whoever shall give to drink a cup of cold water to one of these little ones only in the name of a disciple, truly I say to you he shall not lose his reward.' In my current local context (a rather comfortable, middle-class English parish), we encourage young people to reflect Christ's imperative here by engaging, physically and spiritually, in an annual Slum Survivor project. Through their sacrificial living for a weekend, the young people raise money for overseas aid projects. However, that same Christ-imperative took on an entirely different meaning a few years back when I was working with youth workers from Lebanon. During the 2006 war with Israel, Christian youth workers were housing and feeding displaced Muslim refugees in their country. Both activities seek to be truly Christlike – but that looks different according to the cultural setting.

Christology is a living tradition, explored and developed through creed and council, creative interpretation and cultural conversation. Our task, as ministers of the gospel, is to continue that conversation and interpret Christ for today. Certainly, we must be faithful to the Gospels and the tradition of faith. But we must also be creative and responsive to the needs and expressions of our culture.

The period of history in which we currently live is characterized by an overlap of cultural waves. Modernity is rubbing shoulders with postmodernity and this transition has a fundamental impact on the way we approach Christology. Three main ideas are predominant here.

First, there is a challenge to the very notion of knowledge and truth. Modernity was founded on the idea that objective truths existed, that there were truths to be discovered, and that through logic, research and science, these objective truths could be objectively known. Postmodernity has challenged that assumption. Knowledge is no longer seen as objective and neutral. Everybody has a point of view. Every point of view is equally valid. 'Truth' is pursued at a much more subjective level. We must, of course, celebrate the positive impact that this has had in giving voice to those who have previously been marginalized as a result of ecclesiastical power play. But we must be careful not to lose the grand narrative of the Christian faith in our desire to liberate the captives and hear the silenced. We must be careful to interpret Christ and not to lose sight of the objective truth that he is 'the way and the truth and the life' (John 14.6).

Second, the cultural wave we are currently riding questions the very concept of 'self'. Modernity had a very strong sense of the individual. If the Cartesian principle, 'I think, therefore I am' can be claimed as the philosophical mantra of modernity, Simon and Garfunkel's identification with a rock or an island must surely be its poetic expression. Postmodernity has challenged that notion of 'self'. It is more common now for people to view themselves like onions, with layers of identity that can be either peeled away or called upon whenever the need arises. Ex-Beatle George Harrison was fond of quoting Mahatma Gandhi's exhortation to, 'Create and preserve the image of your choice'. Third, modernity was built upon the notion of 'meta-narrative'; an overarching and controlling story to the way things are. While we note the evolving atheism of post-Enlightenment thinking, it is true to say that the logic and cohesion of early-modernity was that world history had a definite starting point and that it was moving towards an end-game with God. Everything that happened, either on a personal level or nationally or internationally, had to be interpreted and contextualized within that meta-narrative. The logic of post-modernity does not depend on the reality of a meta-narrative. Indeed, the very opposite is true. The logic of postmodernity is dependent on the fact that there is no central storyline at all! Every event, every decision, every action, every thought needs to be considered only within its own context. Beyond our most basic moral and ethical communitarian obligations, there is no external point of reference. The only story that has meaning for me is my story. The only story that has meaning for you is your story. Our stories are not predetermined. Rather, they are being constructed as we journey through life. In his paper, 'Universal History and Cultural Differences', the great philosopher of postmodernity Jean François Lyotard asked the question, 'Can we continue today to organize the multitude of events that come to us from the world, both the human and the non-human world, by subsuming them beneath the idea of a universal history of humanity?' (1989: 314). The unequivocal answer of postmodernity is 'No'.

Herein lie three of the greatest challenges of postmodernity to our theological systems; a challenge to knowledge and truth, a challenge to the concept of self and a challenge to the very concept of meaning itself. It may be that we find some aspects of these challenges positive and other aspects destructive. But they are challenges just the same and we are forced to reconsider our beliefs in the light of their claims. The impact of these challenges on our ministry is immense – not least with regard to our christological foundations. The challenge of postmodernity forces us to develop a Christology for this age, a Christology for this time and this place. Motivated by a desire to minister effectively, we are forced to develop a Christology that answers the questions that are being asked. To be effective in youth ministry, we must develop a Christology that can speak powerfully as knowledge and truth, a Christology that can defend – or at least help reconstruct – concepts of self, personality and human worth and a Christology that presents Jesus as the Lord of time and not just another individual tossed on the waves of the sea of time. As ministers of the gospel, we are compelled to develop a Christology that is firmly rooted in Scripture but has the flexibility to interact with the culture in which we live and work.

Christ and culture

Any consideration of this topic would be incomplete without reference to H. Richard Niebuhr's seminal work, *Christ and Culture*. Resulting from a series of Alumni lectures given at Austin Presbyterian Theological Seminary in Texas, this 1951 publication has proved to be perhaps the most enduring word on the subject. Niebuhr was concerned to outline five 'types' of relationship between Christ and culture, five positional stances that believers may take in their interaction with the world in which they live. If one were to plot a horizontal line, there would be one extreme position at either end and three mediating positions along the middle.

We will briefly consider Niebuhr's types, and I shall illustrate each one with a potential response I could have made to a particular group of young people I worked with when I was ministering in the East End of London. This group of teenagers would congregate on the front porch of our church each night and smoke marijuana. I sat with them two or three nights a week for a period of two years and developed a positive relationship with them that had many transformative benefits for them, for me and for the local community.

Niebuhr's first type is referred to as 'Christ against culture'. A Christian holding this position perceives the world to be utterly lost and corrupted by sin. Christians are called to follow the heavenly imperative, 'Come out, my people, from her so that you do not have fellowship with her sins' (Revelation 18.4). The 'Christ against culture' type portrays the Church as a community of holiness into which the believer must withdraw. It is an uncompromising position that relentlessly pursues purity. It is a position that may result in the establishment of separate communities, such as the Amish. If I engaged with this group of young people from the 'Christ against culture' position, I would have constantly reprimanded them for their use of marijuana; telling them that it was a sin and God was displeased with their behaviour.

At the furthest extreme from the 'Christ against culture' type is the model of 'Christ of culture'. This position supposes there to be no conflict between Christ and culture. There is deemed to be a harmony between the values of the faith and the moral and ethical pursuits of contemporary culture. Those holding to this position might refer to their country as 'a Christian nation'. If I engaged with the young people from this position, I would never have challenged their use of drugs. Instead, I would have accepted that this was their culture and that God could and would accept them as they are. I would have focused on some other aspect of their behaviour – for example, their loyalty and friendship – and would have celebrated that with them as a shared expression of God's love.

In between 'Christ against culture' and 'Christ of culture', there exist three mediating positions.

The first of these, according to Niebuhr, is the idea of 'Christ above culture'. This position endorses the notion that there is good to be found within human cultures. However, this good is not a result of human endeavour so much as a gift from God. For society to fully comprehend what it has received from God, divine revelation is needed. An example of this type is the Christian who sees good things happening in non-Church cultures and recognizes the presence of God there. Paul in Athens provides a biblical warrant for the 'Christ above culture' position: 'Men, Athenians, in all things I see that you are very religious . . . Whom therefore you worship without knowing, him I proclaim to you' (Acts 17.22–23). Engaging with the group from this position, I would have helped them to understand that their loyalty and friendship together was a gift from God and that I was there to help them recognize the God-giver in their midst.

The second mediating position is 'Christ transforming culture'. The idea underpinning this type is that the whole of culture needs to be converted to Christianity. In order to fulfil the mandate to be 'the light of the whole world' (Matthew 5.14), there is a need for Christians to become involved in every stratum of life – business, politics, education, the arts – in order to 'reclaim' them for Christ. From this position, I would perhaps have tolerated their use of drugs for a while while also celebrating their friendship. After a while, I would begin gently challenging their smoking and trust that God would transform their group culture from within.

Finally, Niebuhr explored the mediating position of 'Christ and culture in paradox'. This type explores the tension in which Christians find themselves living. God has given worldly institutions for a purpose and believers must be prepared to work within and alongside such institutions. These institutions, however, are not perfect and there is inherent within them a paradox of kingdom values and sinful human self-interest. It is this paradox that, in AD 55 (just one year after the infamous Nero became Emperor), enabled Paul to reason, 'Let every soul be subject to authorities above. Indeed, there is no authority if

not from God and those that exist have been instituted of God'
(Romans 13.1). From this perspective, I would have recognized
the goodness of their friendship and co-loyalty but would
have recognized the sinfulness of their drug use. I would have
developed a relationship with them that both celebrated and
challenged in equal measure.

Niebuhr's work is not without its weaknesses. Nor is it the
last word on the relationship between Christ and culture. It does,
however, give us a way into understanding how we can develop
a cultural Christology to underpin our mission and ministry
to youth. What Niebuhr shows us is that there are many ways
of presenting the truths of Christianity – and the truth that is
Jesus Christ – to the cultural group among which we minister.
Rather than presenting a static matrix, Niebuhr's typology
presents us with categories that are not mutually exclusive.

Expressing the gospel message will demand differing christological images to speak into different cultures. Crucially,
each cultural group will need a variety of christological images
at various times. There will be times when we need to present
Christ standing against culture. There will be times when
we need to present Christ transforming culture. There will be
times when we need to present Christ standing above culture.
In different situations, even with the same group of young
people, we will need a flexible Christology that can draw on
the diversity of Scripture and speak into the diversity of that
cultural environment.

Perhaps you are wondering how I ministered to this group
of young people using drugs outside our church! The answer
is that I proactively and consciously worked my way through
Niebuhr's model. For the first few months of working with
them, I never criticized this activity. Eventually, when I felt
more secure in my relationship with them, I presented them
with Christ standing against that cultural activity. I quickly
supplemented that with Christ above their culture, encouraging
them to find the good within their chosen lifestyle – loyalty to

each other, laughter, friendship, mutual support through the challenges many faced in education and family instability. From that, we were able to have conversations that explored the Christ and culture in paradox type; the tension between their behavioural patterns and the values of the kingdom of God. I would like to conclude this illustration by saying that the young people all became Christians and renounced their former lifestyles. Sadly, I cannot do so! But one of the boys did recognize that a change was required of him and he subsequently came off drugs and became a youth worker. He now works the same streets I did and has a powerful ministry among the young people who have come after him. His story, I believe, is a wonderful example of the Christ who transforms culture.

Modelling Christ for today

Those of us who are called to Christian youth ministry, in whatever format, are called to missionary work. But the work of a missionary is never just to plant our idea of who Christ is into an alien culture. There must always be a degree of interaction between the scriptural witness and the cultural setting. Christology is about creating a suitable balance between 'Christ' and 'culture'.

In doing that, however, we may do well to recognize that the issue is not so much 'Christ and culture' as 'the culture of Christianity and other cultures'. As we minister the gospel to young people, as we develop a Christology with others, we need to be aware that what we are actually doing is introducing them, not just to a person, but also to a Church culture: a culture of Christianity that cannot be avoided. That is not a bad thing. But it does need to be honestly acknowledged. Postmodernity has taken such a strong grasp on society that the expressive culture of traditional Christianity has become an alien concept to many. There is little or no Christian memory, not just among the young, but even those who are now middle-aged. An example of just how far society has lost its Christian memory relates to a friend of mine who took some young people to see *The Passion* by Mel Gibson when it was released in 2004. When they came out of the cinema afterwards, he asked them what they thought of the film. One boy looked rather confused. 'It was OK,' he said hesitantly, 'but why did you take us to see a film about a bloke getting beaten up?'

A new christological approach is desperately needed for today. The call on us is to model a Christ who is relevant in a multi-cultural, multi-faith environment. The call on us is to model a Christ who speaks powerfully within our cultural settings. This is not to say that Niebuhr's typologies have become irrelevant. It is the case, however, that his work, produced over 50 years ago, now needs to be reassessed and developed for a new age. This book hopes to add to that conversation. But the most exciting realization is that this reassessment and development is not coming out of the academy and books so much as from the coalface of practical youth ministry. Wherever we try to discover new and relevant ways of presenting Christ to young people, we are developing the typology matrix by combining biblical studies with cultural studies. Given the fact that youth culture is so fluid, the christological models that we use this week may be different from the models that we use next week. We may need to speak of Christ as brother and friend today but as judge tomorrow. We may need to stress the forgiving love of Jesus this week but draw attention to his claim of lordship over a believer's life next week. When a young person is doing drugs in our church porch, Christ will stand against that culture. When that young person seeks drug rehabilitation, Christ will transform that culture. When that young person sets up a drug rehabilitation service for other addicts in the neighbourhood, Christ is the fulfiller of that culture.

A prophetic christological model is needed. We are called to be prophets, preparing the way for Christ in our culture. In doing that, we need to develop a Christology that will be flexible enough to discern the need and recognize the movement of God. For that reason, we must work from a *kairos*-perspective. Only a *kairos*-perspective enables us to 'be in the moment' and respond in a flexible way to the immediate situation that confronts us. As youth ministers, we have spent the quiet hours before the day began going deep with God. We have aligned ourselves to him and are finely attuned to the eternal quality contained within each moment of *chronos*-activity. Then, when we encounter a pastoral situation, we are quickly able to see it for what it is – an opportunity to breathe Christ into that moment – and respond as flexibly as we need to, presenting the Christ-image that is required. If we are operating solely out of *chronos*, we will miss the moment because we are not attuned to its potential eternal significance. By the time we have gone through the internal process of seeking Christ, the moment may have passed. Effective ministry can only happen when our focus is on *kairos* rather than *chronos*. That is why effective youth ministry is born out of the regularity of spiritual discipline.

Christology that is based in the *kairos*-moment is not just about studying and knowing the historicity of a man so that we can present the facts to young people when the opportunity arises. *Kairos*-based christological ministry has a social dimension by which the oppressed are free, the captives are released, organizations are reformed and the values of the kingdom of God are instituted. It is a Christology both loyal to Scripture and culturally relevant that will empower the Jesus community to help others move into a life of freedom and healing.

Our commission is awesome. Recognizing the types presented to us by Niebuhr, we are commissioned to strive for purity, to affirm what is good in culture and take every opportunity we have to transform and convert that culture to the glory of God. We acknowledge the paradox that arises from living in the end times – the era of the 'now' and the 'not yet'. But we move out to minister in the power of the greatest christological promise of all: 'I am with you all the days until the completion of the age' (Matthew 28.20).

Pause for thought

- Who is Jesus for you?
- What theological, cultural or political expressions have been the primary influences on the development of your own Christology?
- How do you portray Jesus to your young people? What images or words do you use most frequently, for example, friend, judge, brother, Saviour, Lord, and so on?
- Which images of Christ do you neglect? Why?
- Are there passages of Scripture you avoid using with young people? Why?

2

An incarnational ministry

The most popular concept that has been used – even over-used – to describe effective Christian youth ministry in recent years is that of 'incarnational ministry'. The notion, as we have already noted, is based on the belief that the principle of how Jesus ministered 2000 years ago in Palestine can and should be applied to how we seek to minister to young people in the twenty-first century. We are to become, as Luther said so eloquently in *The Freedom of a Christian* and C. S. Lewis affirmed in *Mere Christianity*, 'little Christs'. As the Word became flesh, so we are to 'flesh the Word' in our own ministerial context.

Many books have been written, many articles posted on the Internet, to explain the concept and explore its implications for contemporary cultural missiology (Google it and see!) Richard Passmore, in his book *Meet Them Where They're At* (2003), is perhaps the most pragmatic exponent of this view. Pete Ward, in *Youthwork and the Mission of God* (1997) and Danny Brierley in *Joined Up* (2003) both explore the same idea. These books, which are predominantly practice-oriented, have been joined by Andy Root's *Revisiting Relational Youth Ministry* (2007).

While contemporary thinking about this topic has many useful insights for youth workers, few authors have avoided sliding into one of two dangerous errors concerning incarna-tional youth ministry. The first of these was explored fully in the Introduction to this book; that we have assumed incarna-tional ministry to be reliant on *chronos*-time – the ability to spend extended periods with young people in order to 'earn the right' to proclaim the gospel. The second error is far more nuanced and, it seems to me, far more theologically erroneous and therefore serious. This is the inability of some writers to distinguish clearly between the person of Christ and the person of the Holy Spirit. We shall address this issue in real depth in Chapter 5. But at this stage, we note the problems that arise when authors write of 'the continuing presence of Christ' with young people. This results in two fundamental crises. First, the youth worker feels that, in some sense, she needs to 'be Christ' to the young person by sharing place with them. As we shall see below, this is not only theologically erroneous in the extreme; it is also a sure-fire recipe for guilt, despondency, low self-esteem and burnout. Second, and just as serious, is the fact that teaching a 'continuing presence of Christ' borders on departure from orthodox Christian belief. As we shall see in a later chapter, Christ is no longer present with us. The Holy Spirit is present with us. If we do not distinguish between these two persons, we nullify Trinitarian belief and therefore contradict credal affirmation. In what follows, I do not want to disparage incarnational youth ministry. Rather, I want to rescue the concept from the promotion of both bad practice and poor, even unorthodox, theology.

Practising incarnation

The fact that the Word became incarnate and assumed human form is the fundamental *raison d'être* for the Church to seek 'the form' of contemporary cultural expression in its effort to relay the good news which is the Christian gospel. For the contemporary Church, this is a foundational principle and underpins all our efforts to be culturally relevant to young people in a postmodern era. To no small extent, the issue is primarily one of initiative. God took the initiative in assuming cultural identity through Christ and so we are to take the initiative in developing ministerial and ecclesiological forms that identify with the shifting patterns of contemporary society. It is no longer enough to assume that the world will come to us. It is no longer enough to assume that we should go to the world. The Church is concerned to blur – even dismantle – the distinctions between 'us' and 'them' in an honest endeavour to present a Christ for today. This is no mere intellectual exercise. It is not enough to *think* as 'they' do: the Church must actively choose to operate beyond its own boundaries – beyond the safety of its own walls – in order to be fully incarnational. The Fresh Expressions movement in the United Kingdom has gone some way towards promoting this mindset in the mainstream Churches. The Emerging Church movement has been somewhat less successful in this endeavour, despite early green shoots and signs of promise a decade or so ago.

It is an often-expressed criticism of contemporary churches that are actively engaged with the young that, in blurring or dismantling the distinctions, the *content* of the gospel is lost through the changing *context* of presentation. This need not necessarily be the case, however. In the same way that Jesus did not deny his divinity in assuming human form, neither need the Church deny its eternal ontological holiness in becoming culturally relevant. In *The Purpose Driven Church*, Rick Warren states,

> Fulfilling God's purpose must always take priority over preserving tradition. If you are serious about ministering to people the way Jesus did, don't be surprised if some of today's religious establishment accuse you of selling out to culture and breaking traditions.
> (1995: 238)

Holding the balance is, of course, difficult and some churches make themselves an easy target by sometimes getting the balance wrong. However, no journey towards self-expression is without its pitfalls and dangers and, just because we sometimes get it wrong, there is no need to abandon that journey. Indeed, if John Stott, writing in *The Contemporary Christian*, is right, we dare not abandon that journey:

On the one hand, [Jesus] came to us in our world, and assumed the full reality of our humanness ... He fraternised with the common people and they flocked around him eagerly ... He identified himself with our sorrows, our sins and our death. On the other hand, in mixing freely with people like us, he never sacrificed, or even for one moment compromised, his own unique identity. His was the perfection of 'holy worldliness'. And now he sends us out into the world as he was sent into the world (John 17.18, 20.21). We have to penetrate other people's worlds, as he penetrated ours – the world of their thinking (as we struggle to understand their misunderstandings of the gospel), the world of their feeling (as we try to empathize with their pain), and the world of their living (as we sense the humiliation of their social situation). (1993: 244)

For the Church to be motivated towards an incarnational ministry, it must, like Jesus before us, be motivated by love. Furthermore, that love – to be truly incarnational – must be unconditional. This is not to suggest soft love but hard love. It will be hard for Christians to love and love and love again even when they face rejection. Furthermore, Christians must be willing to challenge young people without condemning them. Soft love, if it is to be truly incarnational, can never be an option. But grounded in *kairos* as we seek to be, we will be better able to live out of the eternal quality and experience of grace such that it becomes the core of who we are. Then, in each encounter where grace is required, we will no longer be trying to *do* grace; instead, we shall *embody* grace.

Many who write about incarnational youth ministry suggest that the methodology is fundamentally about friendship. I am in agreement with that. However, I suggest that friendship that is based in *chronos* is a friendship that we 'do' to others. That is to say, the friendship we offer to young people is measured in the quantity of time that we spend with them or the effort we put into resolving their problems. Friendship that is born out of *chronos* can only lead to guilt and low self-esteem as the youth worker realizes there just are not enough hours in the day to be 'friends' with all the young people who need her friendship. A friendship that has *kairos*-awareness as its foundation recognizes that *chronos*-activity is not a suitable measure at all. Instead, friendship with a young person is about filling whatever short moment you have to share with an eternal quality. I learnt this from a youth worker called David, before I was a Christian, when I was persuaded by my Christian sister to go on a Christian residential. David was constantly in demand from the 200 young people there. I never had more than five minutes with him on any given occasion. But, for those five minutes, his eye contact never wavered and he listened intently to what I had to say. On each occasion, David made me feel like the only person in the room. That was true friendship. That was *kairos*-friendship – and my understanding of God was transformed by his attentiveness to me.

The witness of the Gospels to us is that Jesus was prepared to be the true friend of sinners. Jesus at a wedding; Jesus having dinner with his friends; Jesus out for a walk on the beach or in the cornfields; Jesus sending up the Pharisees and the rich; Jesus telling tall stories; Jesus mocking the system. Even though each social encounter was brief, Jesus sought to *live* the gospel message by embodying the friendship of God to sinners. He was never with any one sinner, or group of sinners, for very long. He was always moving on. Yet each encounter was a *kairos*-friendship that transformed the lives of those he met.

A saying erroneously attributed to Francis of Assisi is valuable for us: 'Preach the Gospel always. Only use words if you have to.' Embodiment, through *kairos*-friendship, is often more powerful than words. That is the testimony of true incarnational ministry.

Beyond incarnation

There is little doubt about the validity of this biblical model for ministry. Which one of us would deny the power of *kairos*-relationships in the presentation of the gospel? Which one of us would deny the need to embody the gospel in this way? But the truth is that, for many of us, incarnation has become a methodology we try to practise rather that a lifestyle we embrace. So how do we develop *kairos*-incarnation rather than *chronos*-incarnation? Or put another way, what does incarnational youth ministry look like when it is a spiritual practice rather than a methodology?

It is in Philippians 2.5–11 that we see this truth expounded most graciously. This passage, of course, is not so much about Jesus as it is about you and me! Paul begins in verse 5 by stating, 'Let this mind be in you, which also was in Christ Jesus'. Christ is the exemplar but we are the objects of Paul's concern here. In the verses that follow, Paul outlines the true cost of an incarnational ministry:

> Let this mind be in you, which also was in Christ Jesus:
> Who subsisting in the form of God
> did not esteem equality with God as something to be
>   grasped
> but emptied himself
> having taken the form of a servant
> having become in the likeness of men;
> and having been found in the outward appearance of a
>   man
> he humbled himself having become obedient unto death
> moreover, death of the cross.

If we are to move '*beyond* incarnation' as a *chronos*-based methodology and '*into* incarnation' as a *kairos*-based spiritual discipline in our youth ministry, we need to briefly unpack this passage to find out what it may entail.

Abandonment of equality

> He did not esteem equality with God as something to be
>   grasped

As we have suggested earlier, the history of the institutional Church in the Constantinian era is imbued with the meta-narrative of power. This book is no place to argue the point nor go into details: the truth is self-evident. A system of rights and privileges is what has given power to the priesthood and/or presbyteral system, in terms of both personal and doctrinal authority. Sometimes, though not always, this has had negative implications and results. Nevertheless, power and position have traditionally gone hand in hand with the proclamation of the gospel.

According to this christological exposition in Paul's letter to the Philippians, this was not the way of Christ. For him, the notion of relying on power and privilege was not an option in the act of incarnation. Perhaps Jesus could have claimed equality with God, quite literally, as his divine right. But he chose not to do so. Indeed, as Alec Motyer points out in *The Message of Philippians* (1984: 110), there may also be two other interpretations of this sentence which would carry even more profound overtones. First, that Jesus would not cling on to a position that could be exploited for self-advantage. Second, that equality could be grasped as a thief steals something that does not belong to him.

Incarnational ministry, after the model of Christ, begins with the foundational ideal that powers and privileges must not be claimed. We may have the 'right' to the benefits of a particular office but that does not mean that we should necessarily claim them. Far less should we fall into the temptation of exploiting position and power for self-gain. The temptations for those in youth ministry are very real. We must pray for ourselves and for those in ecclesial authority for wisdom in the way we and they use the authority that God has given.

This, of course, is something of a paradox for all of us involved in youth work. The last couple of decades have been dedicated to the professionalization of youth ministry throughout the Western world. This drive has resulted in better training, better housing, more equitable pay scales, the creation of trade unions for youth workers and the formation of professional bodies to support those who are involved in practical ministry as well as those who provide training. It is perhaps the case that, more so than ever before, youth workers are aware of their 'rights' as well as their 'responsibilities'.

I am certainly not arguing for a de-professionalization of Christian youth ministry. I have dedicated the best part of my ministry to developing accredited training courses for youth workers as well as proactively advocating for better working conditions, on a par with other recognized church ministerial positions. I am the last person to advocate a return to the dark ages, when youth workers were paid a pittance, given a damp flat to live in, expected to work 60 hours a week, shown where the local council estate was and told by the church elders, 'There's the mission field – off you go. Our thoughts and prayers are with you!' But I am suggesting that there is a difference between enjoying the benefits of being a professional (which is good) and the claiming of power and authority that naturally arises from that position (which is bad).

Not all rights are right! Human rights are right – the right to a decent wage and suitable housing, for example – and it is entirely appropriate for a youth worker to expect these rights to be met. I am not suggesting that this passage from Philippians is a call to abandon human rights. However, there are some rights that are wrong. I know of one church where the staff team has reserved parking places outside the church. Why should they have that privilege when the elderly are struggling through the rain and snow to come to Sunday worship? I know another church where, without permission being given, each church member is put on a rota to do the gardening, cleaning and even Sunday cooking for the youth worker. The vicar sends them a letter of reprimand if they do not turn up on their appointed day. That right strikes me as being very wrong!

We must be sure that we cling to the right rights and not the wrong rights.

Abandonment of self

but emptied himself

One of the most disputed aspects of theology has been the notion of kenotic Christology; the idea from this verse in Philippians that Christ 'emptied' himself. As Paul says, rather than claiming his power and privileges, Jesus chose to give them up. The question of kenotic Christology is, 'What does it mean for Jesus to have emptied himself? Did he somehow become less than he was?' However, as Motyer suggests, this may not be the question we need to ask.

> We ought to notice that in asking the perfectly natural question, 'Of what did Christ empty himself,' we are, in fact, departing from the direct line of thought in this passage . . . It is not 'Of what did he empty himself?' but 'Into what did he empty himself?'
> (1984: 113)

It is easy for us to forget the privilege of Christian ministry. I have been involved in the training of hundreds of youth workers through the years, and it has always been a sadness to me to see some of them leaving college more cynical about their calling than when they arrived. Certainly, there are many sacrifices we are called to make as ministers of the gospel, whether full-time or part-time, paid or volunteer. We sacrifice our time and our ambition. There is also often a cost to family time and potential salary. It is not unusual, or inappropriate, for us to have moments when we feel thoroughly 'poured out'. It seems to me that the only way to prevent disillusion and/or burnout is to re-frame the experience. We are not being poured out so much as being poured into. Rather than the image of a jug of water being emptied out, we need instead to picture the water being poured *into something*. It is that *something* that makes sense of this passage and, ultimately, our calling.

Acceptance of servant status

having taken the form of a servant

And that *something* is the something of servanthood. Complete and utter self-giving. As Gordon Fee says in *Philippians*, 'This is how divine love manifests itself in its most characteristic and profuse expression. Christ entered our history not as *kyrios* ("Lord") . . . but as *doulos* ("slave"), a person without advantages, rights or privileges, but in servanthood to all' (2010: 95).

Crucially, Jesus is the servant of all. He did not pick and choose whom he served. He was the servant of all. That is the hard part of ministry in and for the Christian Church – to be the servant of all. The temptation for those in Christian youth ministry is often to fall into one or more errors with regard to servanthood.

First, we are tempted to be choosy about whom we decide to serve. It is often the case that our churches exist for the acceptable and shun the unacceptable. When I was vicar of a church a number of years ago in the East End of London, a bag-lady began attending our Sunday evening worship. After one month, a small group of respectable ladies, who had been regular worshippers for many years, came to me with an ultimatum. They brought my attention to the severe body odour problem which the bag-lady had (as if I hadn't noticed it myself!) and then proceeded to say, 'You need to make a choice, vicar. This woman is ruining our worship. You must either ask her to leave the church or we won't be back!'

For a while, I missed this group of ladies . . . but not for too long.

Second, we are tempted to be servants – but not as an end in itself. We may choose to serve our young people *in order that* they are converted to the faith. We may choose to serve our young people *in order that* they will find new friends within the family of the Church. We may choose to serve our young people *in order that* we grow the size of our youth group. We may not be consciously aware of these driving forces but we must examine our hearts and our motivations. Such conditional service is not the way of Christ. He served. Full stop. Christ became the servant of all and continued to serve even when the majority did not choose to recognize him. Jesus never served *in order that* . . . Jesus just served.

Acceptance of identification

having become in the likeness of men; and having been found in the outward appearance of a man

Contrary to Docetic views (the idea that Jesus only *appeared* to be fully human), the Incarnation was full, real and complete. When people came into contact with Jesus, they came into contact with a man. To be sure, there is an ambiguity about this verse ('having become in the likeness of men; and having been found in the outward appearance of a man') that allows for the fact that this was no ordinary man. Jesus was one of us – and yet different. The God-Man embraces human culture and yet still remains above it. In the same way, we are called to a form of ministry that embraces the culture in which we live and work and yet remain somehow detached from it. We are called to be 'in the world but not of it'. We are to be Jews when we are with Jews, Gentiles when we are with Gentiles. We are to be all things to all people so that we may win some for Christ. The hardest part of this incarnational ministry that we are called to practise is holding in tension this paradox of cultural embracing–detachment in such a way that we remain authentic in love. As Stott commented, 'In every non-Christian (and many Christians too), even in the jolliest extroverts, there are hidden depths of pain. We can reach them only if we are willing to enter into their suffering' (1993: 360). It is no easy task to enter into suffering in the way that Jesus does. However, nothing less is required of us in Christian youth ministry.

There is, of course, a tension that youth workers must work with in modelling this aspect of christological ministry. We are to *embrace* youth culture without ever pretending that we are *part of* youth culture. If we get the balance wrong, we are in danger of undoing our good work. For three years in the 1990s, I worked with a tough group of young people on a housing estate near Birmingham. After a while, we decided to open up a coffee bar for them one night a week in our church. I remember being so concerned that this should be a success that I planned the opening night of this brave new venture down to every last meticulous detail. As these suspicious teenagers crossed the threshold into our coffee bar, I turned up the music CD I had bought that week – a collection of Rave tracks. The young people sat there all evening, chatting quietly. As we closed the coffee bar at the end of the night, I asked a couple of boys if they had had a good time. They shuffled their feet nervously. One of them spoke up.

'Yeah, it was OK. But . . .' his voice trailed off.

'But what?' I asked curiously.

'Well . . . it was really good . . . but . . . but next time, could we bring our *own* music?'

I learnt my lesson! Incarnational ministry does not require of us to appear trendy and cool if we are not trendy and cool! I thought I understood their culture and could provide the right music. I did not really understand their culture at all. Authenticity is all-important. As youth workers, we are called to be *in* their world without trying to be *of* their world.

A controlled life

he humbled himself having become obedient

The Gospel narratives portray the image of a man who was utterly reliant on his Father. Jesus was completely obedient to God in regard to his activities (John 5.19), in regard to his judgements (John 5.30) and in regard to his speaking (John 8.28). Obedience is the model that Jesus gives us and obedience to the Father God is the teaching that he gives us through the Sermon on the Mount: obedience in conduct (Matthew 5.15, 44, 48; 6.1), prayer (Matthew 6.8, 9; 7.11) and daily reliance on him (Matthew 6.31, 32).

We noted in the Introduction that personal spirituality is the foundation for an effective Christian youth ministry. At the heart of personal spirituality is obedience. In an effort to be culturally relevant, it is a grave mistake to jettison our commitment to modelling obedience to God for the young people whom we are called to serve. It is a sad indictment on the state of the Christian faith today, so deeply unattractive to so many young people, that it is no longer perceived to be a cause worth living for, let alone dying for.

If we are to learn one thing from the rise of religious fundamentalism among young people in our societies today, it is surely that obedience to a cause is seen as an attractive option. Not only is that true of fundamentalism. Islam, Buddhism and Hinduism are all increasing in popularity and each one of these has spiritual discipline at its heart. As a vicar in a predominantly Muslim area of east London, I was often confronted with the chasm that existed between the Christian witness and that of the local Islamic community. Never was that chasm more starkly pronounced than on Friday nights. Opposite the vicarage in which I lived, there was a small road junction. On one side was a pub. On the other side was a mosque. At ten o'clock each Friday night, I would look out my window and see two contrasting cultures exhibited. On one pavement, young white men would be spilling out of the doors, drunk, loud and abusive. On the other pavement, young Muslim boys would quietly file out of the mosque, Qur'an in hand, after an evening of prayer and worship. The difference between the two cultures could not have been more pronounced. The fallacy that young people are not attracted to a life of obedience is just that. If the cause is right, young people will be obedient. The challenge facing youth ministers today is to portray Christianity as a just cause, worth living and dying for. We will not be able to rise to that challenge unless we are convinced ourselves and are prepared to live accordingly.

I am not arguing a case for blind, unquestioning obedience. We have all seen too many lives destroyed by the spiritual abuse that precedes or results in the demand for unthinking submission. Neither am I suggesting that the call to obedience somehow fulfils the need we all have for certainty in our lives. But I do want to suggest that the notion of obedience needs to be redeemed from the negative connotations that so often surround it in contemporary society. Paul argues in Galatians that obedience is the path to fullness of life and authenticity as human beings:

> For freedom you were called, brothers; only do not use the freedom as a pretext for the flesh, but through love become slaves to one another. For the whole law is fulfilled in one word, 'You shall love your neighbour as yourself'.   (Galatians 5.13, 14)

Obedience is the path to freedom.

A controlled death

> having become obedient unto death
> moreover, death on the cross

Paul stresses the incredible depth of Jesus' commitment to humanity by the repetition of the word 'death' in this verse. His commitment was total, as Fee reminds us:

47

No one in Philippi, we must remind ourselves, used the cross as a symbol for their faith; there were no gold crosses embossed on Bibles or worn as pendants around the neck or lighted on the steeple of the local church. The cross was God's – and thus their – scandal, God's contradiction to human wisdom and power: that the One they worshiped as Lord should have been crucified as a state criminal at the hands of one of 'lord' Caesar's proconsuls; that the Almighty should appear in human dress, and that he should do so in this way, as a messiah who died by crucifixion. Likewise, this is the scandal of Pauline ethics: that the God who did it this way 'gifts' us to 'suffer for his sake' in this way as well.

(2010: 97)

And that is the ultimate call of Christian ministry; that we must be prepared to die to self (literally or metaphorically). It is, of course, a scandal even today. It is a scandal to an institution that it is called to renounce all power and privilege. It is a scandal to the rich and the spiritually powerful that we are called to assume the form of servants – without question and without motive. It is a scandal that the body of Christ is called to give up everything that it has in order to model Christ.

It is a scandal to a traditional Church that it is called to die.

Ultimately, however, that is what incarnational ministry is all about. We belittle the concept if we continue to think about it merely in terms of building relationships and making ourselves culturally relevant. Incarnational ministry is as much about death as it is about life. It will be a courageous – and obedient – Church that seeks to model this form of ministry into the twenty-first century. Is the contemporary Church brave enough to rise to that challenge and pave the way for a truly incarnational transformation of society?

I believe that those of us who are involved in youth ministry are called to a prophetic ministry. We are called to be prophets to the young people among whom we live and minister. But we are also called to be prophets to the Church. A prophetic youth ministry will teach the Church how to die well so that others may live. Then, and only then, will we be truly incarnational in our approach.

Pause for thought

- How do you enter the world of pain that some of your young people inhabit?
- What does it mean for you to offer friendship to the young people you serve? How does that friendship manifest itself?
- What are the right rights for you to claim and what are the wrong rights that you must reject in your life?
- How do you cope when feeling that you are being poured out? What is God pouring you into?
- What does obedience look like in your life? What should it look like?
- What aspects of your Church should die? What aspects of your own life should die?

3

A crucified ministry

The crucifixion of Jesus stands at the very heart of the Christian faith. Ours is a crucified Lord. The validity of the gospel stands or falls on the death and resurrection of Jesus. As Paul wrote, 'I delivered to you in the first place what I received, that Christ died for our sins, according to the Scriptures and that he was buried and that he was raised on the third day according to the Scriptures' (1 Corinthians 15.3, 4). If Christ had not died and was not raised, there would be no Christian faith.

Since our ministry is to model that of Jesus, and since the crucifixion was so central to his ministry, then we must assume that his death has much to teach us about how we can minister to others. The simple truth is this: those involved in Christian youth ministry are called to die. Dietrich Bonhoeffer, in his *Ethics*, distilled that wonderful soundbite, 'When Christ calls a man, he bids him come and die.' What does that mean in the context of our youth ministry? The answer is given in Mark 9.35: 'If anyone wishes to be first, he must be last of all and servant of all.'

Christian youth ministry is hallmarked, theologically, by death. It is only when we learn to die that we learn to live. So it is, then, that when we learn to die, so we are better able to minister to others. That is the example of Christ to us. That is the ministry of Christ *to* us. Our task in this chapter is to explore the notion of a crucified Christology, the idea that our ministry must be modelled on that of the Christ who was crucified. In exploring this idea, we will work through three stages. First, we must think through exactly why Jesus had to die. Second, we will consider why it is that death to self is the ultimate expression of *kairos*-ministry. Finally, we will explore how this crucified ministry of Christ can serve as a model as we minister to young people by focusing on the words of Jesus from the cross recorded in the Gospel of Luke.

Why did Christ have to die?

The crucifixion of Jesus Christ is the pivotal event in Scripture. The whole of his life, teaching and ministry was building up to that moment. We can make sense of the resurrection, Ascension and second coming only in the light of the tragedy of Good Friday. In comprehending the magnitude of the event in terms of a christological model for ministry, we are bound to start with the most basic question of all: why did Jesus have to die? Finding an answer to that question is not as easy as it may seem. There are a number of different, equally valid, answers – both historical and theological.

Historically, we may argue that Jesus Christ was put to death because he had upset the religious and political authorities. The narrative of the people of Israel running through the Old Testament era – and the subsequent story that unfolded through the book of Acts – portrays God as an intensely 'political' God. So it is not surprising that the death of Jesus should be an intensely political death. First, it was the intent of the Roman authorities to execute Jesus. The form of execution they chose was the most terrible form of punishment and humiliation, reserved only for the most hardened criminals, for slaves and for political agitators. It was in the latter category that Jesus was placed. The Roman authorities viewed him as a political threat, upsetting the *status quo* and undermining the fabric of society in Jerusalem through a programme of non-violent resistance. However, the situation was considerably more complex than that because Pontius Pilate did not perceive Jesus as a serious menace. He knew that the Jewish spiritual authorities were merely using the Roman legal system for their own ends.

Pilate wanted to protect himself from the wrath of the Emperor and was therefore willing to put power-games and politics before justice. For Pilate, the real political issue was why the rabbis and chief priests wanted Jesus dead.

To understand exactly why the Jewish authorities wanted to pursue this course of action, we need to locate Jesus within the tradition of the prophets. That is clearly how the people of Israel, among whom he was ministering, were interpreting Jesus. In Matthew 16.14, Peter acknowledges that 'Some say [you are] John the Baptist, and others Elijah, and others Jeremiah or some other prophet'. After Jesus raised the widow's son in Nain, the observers of that miracle exclaimed, 'A great prophet has risen up among us!' (Luke 7.16). Likewise, the adoring crowd heralded the triumphal entry into Jerusalem with the claim, 'This is the prophet Jesus, from Nazareth in Galilee' (Matthew 21.11). During the week of Jesus' Passion, we read of the Pharisees that, 'seeking to lay hold of him, they feared the crowds because they held him as a prophet' (Matthew 21.46). Furthermore, when the risen Christ appeared to the two men on the road to Emmaus, they spoke to the mysterious companion of '[Jesus of Nazareth] who was a man, a prophet mighty in works and word before God and all the people' (Luke 24.19). Crucially, it would seem that Jesus' self-understanding was partly founded on the idea of him being the latest in a long line of prophets. After having been rejected at Nazareth, Jesus commented that, 'A prophet is not without honour except in his home town and among his relatives and in his household' (Mark 6.4). Since Jesus is located within that prophetic tradition, we are not surprised that his ministry incorporated the key characteristics of Israel's prophetic tradition. Most important for our purposes is Jesus' use of symbolic action.

Integral to the prophetic ministry was the performance of some symbolic act to bring home the importance of the word they were bringing from God. Often, that symbolic act would make reference to, or be performed at, the Temple. Jeremiah declared the need for repentance at the gate of the Temple (Jeremiah 7.1). Joel exhorted the leaders of Judah to gather at the Temple for prayer and petition (Joel 1.14). Upon the return from exile in Babylon, Haggai presented the remnant with a word from the Lord, 'Is it time [*kairos*] for you to dwell in your fine houses when our house [the Temple] is desolate?' (Haggai 1.4). God spoke through Malachi to present the people with the same spiritual reality, 'An abomination has occurred in Israel and in Jerusalem, because Judah has profaned the holy things of the Lord, which he loves' (Malachi 2.11).

With regard to the religious authorities wanting to execute Jesus, perhaps the critical moment was when he went to the Temple and overturned the tables of the moneylenders. This act, recorded in all four Gospels, presents Jesus as standing within the prophetic tradition. His actions on that fateful day symbolically portrayed his belief that the Temple was under judgement. By implication, the leaders of the Jewish religious community were under judgement too. As Jesus overturned the tables, he was inviting his hearers to join him in purifying the Jewish religion and thereby establish the true Temple. For the religious leaders, Jesus' cleansing of the Temple was the final act that would crystallize their thinking. The false prophet had to go. So it was that the Roman and Jewish leaders conspired to kill Jesus under the banner, 'The King of the Jews' (Mark 15.26). This, of course, is the greatest irony about the crucifixion of Jesus. In proclaiming him King of the Jews, the Roman and Jewish authorities inadvertently announced the theological reality that underpinned his death: the kingdom of God.

Jesus recognized a purpose in his death that would go beyond any immediate historical explanation. He understood his life and ministry – and even his own death – in terms of restoring and renewing the covenant relationship that existed between God and humanity. He knew that, through his death, forgiveness of sins would be won for all who trusted in him. He was sure that his death would make effective reconciliation between humanity and God. On the night before he died, at supper with his friends, he had declared the cup to be symbolic of 'the new covenant in my blood, which is poured out for you' (Luke 22.20).

Within a very few years of his death, many first-century Jews had grasped the theological implications of the crucifixion. There is an abundance of images used in the New Testament letters to describe exactly what it was that Jesus achieved on the cross. Just a few examples will suffice.

One such motif for Paul was the idea of reconciliation between God and humanity. So, in his letter to the Romans, Paul states that, 'We boast in God through our Lord Jesus Christ through whom now we have received reconciliation' (5.11). Again, to the believers in Corinth, Paul writes that, 'God was in Christ reconciling the world to himself' (2 Corinthians 5.19). That friendship is made effective through interchange as we participate in the death of Christ and he carries our sinful nature: 'The one not having known sin for us he made sin, in order that we may become the righteousness of God in him' (2 Corinthians 5.21).

The Gospel writers use a wide variety of images to describe the theological impact of the crucifixion. The Synoptic Gospels portray Jesus' self-understanding on the matter with such theological foci as the idea of ransom: 'For even the son of man did not come to be served but to serve and give his life as a ransom for many' (Mark 10.45).

Not surprisingly, the Gospel of John draws on a richer vein of symbolic and spiritual images. The writer sees meaning in the fact that 'it is necessary for the son of man to be lifted up' (3.14), and that the crucifixion would be the source of glory (7.39).

In the letter to the Hebrews, Jesus' death on the cross is related to the Old Testament images of sacrifice (9.14; 9.26; 10.9; 10.12; 13.20).

Peter draws on his Jewish heritage too in exploring the meaning of the crucifixion. In 1 Peter 1.18–19, he reminds his readers that, 'you were redeemed from the futile manner of your life handed down by your fathers by precious blood as of a lamb without blemish and without spot, of Christ'. As that sacrificial lamb, 'Christ himself bore our sins in his body on the tree' (1 Peter 2.24). In accordance with the Pauline motif of interchange, Peter acknowledges that, 'Christ once for sins suffered, the righteous for the unrighteous' (1 Peter 3.18).

Clearly, the crucifixion of Jesus Christ is a historical event laden with complexity. There are so many different ways to interpret what happened that Friday afternoon on a hill outside of Jerusalem 2000 years ago. Yet conversely, the crucifixion of Jesus Christ is also amazingly simple. It remains the greatest symbol of God standing with his hurting and damaged creation. It will forever be the ultimate testimony of God's love for a broken people. It is that simplicity that is mirrored as we reflect a crucified Christology in our own ministry to others.

Death to self and *kairos*-ministry

We have already identified *kairos* as the experience of eternal quality within a *chronos*-moment. *Kairos* is the quality or meaning that inhabits *chronos*, enjoyed as a moment of meaning with another individual, or creation, or God. It may be fleeting in terms of *chronos*, but it is of eternal value in terms of *kairos* because *kairos*, by definition, is only measurable by eternal value.

In Mark 8.34–35 Jesus exhorts his disciples,

> If anyone desires to follow after me, let him disown himself and let him take up his cross and let him follow me. For whoever wishes to save his life will lose it; and whoever loses his life for my sake, and for the gospel, will save it.

In Romans 6.6, Paul writes, 'We know that our old man was crucified with him in order that the body of sin might be destroyed.' An analysis of these verses from the Greek leads us into a deeper understanding of the relationship between death to self and the formation of a *kairos*-ministry.

In Mark 8.34, there are three verbs – 'disown', 'take up', and 'follow'. The way Mark constructs the Greek verb-tenses in this sentence makes it clear that the primary emphasis is on the notion of following the example of Jesus ('disown' and 'take up' are aorist imperatives while 'follow' is a present imperative). It is our following in the example of Christ that is important. However, that can only happen as we dis-own self and take up our cross, which is a metaphor for dying to self. But that is not to say that dying to self is a 'work' that we can achieve ourselves. Paul makes it clear in Romans 6.6 that we are the passive recipients of death through the death of Christ on the cross: 'Our old man was crucified with him'. Further, the phrase 'might be destroyed' is an aorist passive participle, which means the action achieved in the verb (destruction of the body of sin) is dependent on the action that has happened (the crucifixion of the old man with Christ). Death to self is not a human work but utterly dependent on that which has been achieved for us by Christ on the cross. Our authentic personality is not found in ego – which has been crucified in Christ and has been forsaken when we chose to disown, take up our cross, and follow – but in the new being that has arisen as a result of us being crucified with Christ.

That being the case, the definition of dying to self involves the ceasing of all ego-work and the replacement of this by passive reliance on the work of Christ in our very being. We know that the ego-state is governed by, and can only exist in, the experience of *chronos* and that the actualization of spiritual experience can only exist in *kairos*. So we die to self when we seek to live in *kairos*-time rather than *chronos*-time; when we choose to find eternal meaning within a moment of encounter with God, or creation, or another individual.

This sounds very deep and philosophical! But what does it mean in practice? Let me give a simple example to help illustrate it.

Recently, I was at the Greenbelt Festival. There was a particular speaker I had been looking forward to hearing since his place at the Festival was announced. It would be, for me, the highlight of my weekend. With half an hour before I was due to go to his session, I was finishing my lunch when a young person I knew came and sat with me. She began to talk about a particular crisis in her life. This was an important conversation for her but, for me, it felt like an inconvenience because I wanted to get to the seminar. In the moment of realization, I had a choice to make. I could either give in to my ego-state and go with my own *chronos*-desire ('*I* only have ten minutes, *I* need to get going, *I* want to hear my favourite speaker, *I* want to be fed') or I could try to see this moment as a *kairos*-encounter ('*She* wants to speak, *she* wants to be heard, *she* is looking for understanding, *she* is searching for something deep'). In choosing the latter, I had to die to self and live to her. That was a choice for *kairos* over *chronos*.

This may not seem a particularly profound example. But that is the point! *Kairos*-ministry, in and of itself, is rarely more than a mundane encounter; often very limited in terms of *chronos*-time, and yet it proves to carry the value and weight of eternity within it and therefore is very significant indeed. To minister in *kairos* does not mean that we have to constantly be searching for deep and meaningful encounters. On the contrary, it means that we are able to find, or create, eternal value in each mundane encounter we have.

Viewed from the perspective of *chronos*, the crucifixion of Christ was mundane indeed. Viewed from the perspective of *kairos*, it was the moment of ultimate, cosmic, eternal value. On the cross of Christ, *kairos* completely inhabited *chronos*. The crucifixion of Christ is the ultimate example of *kairos* breaking into, and re-defining, *chronos*. In Romans 6.6, Paul writes, 'We know that our old man was crucified with him in order that the body of sin might be destroyed'. For that reason, developing a truly crucified youth ministry is the ultimate expression of *kairos*-ministry.

But what does it mean in practice to have a crucified ministry?

A crucified ministry

As Jesus was dying on the cross, he uttered seven 'words'. These sayings have an immense value for Christians because they distil the entire teaching canon of Jesus' earthly ministry into short, concentrated sentences. Four are recorded solely in chapter 23 of Luke's Gospel. As we reflect on these four 'words', we can see the fundamental attitudes that underpin a crucified Christology for youth ministry.

Sorrow

> 'Daughters of Jerusalem, do not weep for me; but weep for yourselves and your children.'
>
> (Luke 23.28)

As a vicar in the East End of London, I ministered in a tough, multi-cultural area that was reflected in the diverse congregation of the church. We had a dozen or more nationalities within the church family, mainly from various African nations. Each Wednesday night, we had a prayer meeting. We would have a period of general thanksgiving before focusing on one topic in particular. The most regular to attend the prayer meeting was a young man named Solomon. In his mid-twenties, he had recently moved to England from Nigeria. Solomon was a wonderful man, deeply spiritual, who taught us all so much about discipleship. Most importantly, Solomon had an incredible ministry of intercessory prayer. During the meetings, Solomon would sit with us for the prayers of thanksgiving. However, when we moved into a time of prayer for a particular topic,

Solomon would sit apart from the rest of us and pray in his own way. He cried. Week after week, whatever area of the world we prayed for or whoever we prayed for, Solomon cried. He had an extraordinary ability to see the world through the eyes of God and that concern led him to weep with sorrow. He had no need for words. Solomon's ministry of intercession was rooted in an experience of *kairos*.

The sorrow that Solomon experienced as he reflected on God's creation mirrored the concern that Jesus showed in his earthly ministry. Twice in the Gospels, we are told that Jesus cried. The first time is in Luke 19.41–44 where he weeps over Jerusalem. The second occasion is in John 11.28–37 where Jesus weeps over the death of his dear friend, Lazarus. These two events show the incredible sorrow that would overwhelm Jesus when he was moved by the need and vulnerability of human beings. Even as he was dying, that sense of sorrow never left him. Indeed, it intensified as he thought about the unregenerate people of Jerusalem so wrapped up in their everyday living that they were oblivious to the Saviour dying for them on a hill just beyond the city walls. So he looks upon those women who were weeping for him and points them in the direction of intercessory ministry. 'Daughters of Jerusalem! Do not weep for me, but weep for yourselves and your children' (Luke 23.28).

There can be no greater motivation for us in youth ministry than to be moved by sorrow. The truth is that if we are not moved to sorrow for those around us, we will never be motivated to minister to their needs. From our crucified Lord, we learn that ministry begins with tears as we learn to see the world through God's eyes.

But there is an immense personal cost involved in modelling our ministry on the crucified Lord. There is truth in the old adage, 'Be careful what you pray for. It might just happen!' If we want to follow the example of the crucified Christ, we will feel true sorrow for those to whom we minister. But sorrow hurts. Sorrow is not like a tap that can be switched on and off. Sorrow is not felt only between the hours of 9 and 5. Sorrow does not leave our hearts during the vacation period. Sorrow cuts deep within us and defines who we are. A crucified Christology reveals a Saviour who was motivated completely by sorrow for his creation. That sorrow led him to sacrifice himself for those in need.

If we wish to minister to young people after the example of Jesus Christ, we must be aware of the consequences for us. We will hurt deeply. We will need to forsake personal ambition – maybe even personal happiness – for others. It is a tough calling. Be careful what you pray for. It might just happen.

Sympathy

> 'Father, forgive them, for they do not know what they
> are doing.'
>
> (Luke 23.34)

I have always thought that Job's friends get a bit of a raw deal. Every sermon and almost every book in which I have heard them mentioned comments on them negatively. They are most often portrayed as bumbling fools who are insensitive to Job's pain, trying desperately to justify their God against a man who must have behaved unrighteously to receive such tragedy in his life. I think that is unfair. To be sure, they may not have been great theologians and the advice they gave to Job may have missed the mark somewhat. Nevertheless, they showed extraordinary pastoral sensitivity and great sympathy for Job and we have much to learn from them.

Job 2 introduces the three friends. Eliphaz, Bildad and Zophar lived some distance away, in different cities. On hearing of Job's distressing situation, they 'came to him each from his own country' (verse 11). The fact that they were prepared to leave behind their work and families for their friend is testimony to their sympathetic spirits and depth of love for the man. No doubt there would have been some personal cost involved in such a decision. Drawing near to Job, they did not recognize him at first. When they did, however, 'they cried in a loud voice, wept, and each one ripped their clothes, and sprinkled earth on their heads' (verse 12). What an extraordinary example of sorrow! Here are three men who knew the agonies of intercessory prayer and ministry. And still the most incredible act of sympathy is to come. 'They sat beside him for seven days and nights and none of them spoke; for they saw that his affliction was terrible and great' (verse 13). This is one of the greatest examples of pastoral care in Scripture; one of the greatest examples of *kairos*-ministry. To sit with someone for seven days and nights without saying a word, just feeling their pain, is *kairos*-ministry at its very best. Acting out of love and sympathy, Eliphaz, Bildad and Zophar had come to do two things for Job.

First, they had come to console Job. Two Hebrew words are used in this passage to explore the depth of the sympathy they had for him: *nud* and *ke'eb*. As J. Gerald Janzen comments, the first of these 'refers to a bodily motion of shaking, moving to and fro, nodding the head' (1985: 56). Such is the intensity of their sorrow that no words could possibly describe their feelings: only bodily movements to express their grief and sympathy. The second Hebrew word, *ke'eb*, 'encompasses both mental and physical anguish' (1985: 57). These three friends were not paying lip service to Job. They felt his pain as if it were their own.

Second, they have come to comfort Job. The verb used for 'comfort' in verse 11 is *nhm*. The meaning implied is that the act of comforting will involve changing Job's mind about his circumstances. As Janzen explains,

> It refers to the action (usually the action of speaking) by which one hopes to bring about a change in or hopes to encourage another to effect a change in how that other feels, thinks, and intends concerning a given state of affairs . . . The friends hope to enter deeply with Job into his condition and then to help him come out of it in a manner which enables him to go on with his life in a spirit other than that of perpetual bereavement.
>
> (1985: 57)

Eliphaz, Bildad and Zophar, despite the mistakes they might make later, have an extraordinary ministry in sorrow and sympathy for Job. They understand that both silence and speech are necessary as they seek to minister to their friend. They feel Job's pain as if it were their own and are prepared to sacrifice their own comfort in an attempt to restore Job to physical, spiritual and emotional health. They serve as a wonderful example to us of how important sympathy is in effective Christian youth ministry towards those who hurt.

As Jesus died on the cross, he showed extraordinary sympathy to those who were crucifying him. 'Father, forgive them, for they do not know what they are doing' (Luke 23.34). Even in his agony, Jesus identifies with his torturers and recognizes the blindness that leads them to perpetuate this most awful crime. How easy it would have been to condemn the soldiers and the Sanhedrin for their actions. Crucifying Jesus was a choice they had made. Rather than condemning, however, Jesus pleads to his Father for forgiveness to be offered to them. He recognized their human frailty, he saw them as damaged human beings in bondage to the power of sin. To be sure, they had chosen to crucify Jesus – but such are the choices made by sinful human beings. This supreme act of sympathy came at considerable personal cost to Jesus. As chapter 23 continues, we see that he had to endure much rather than retaliate in anger or self-justification: 'They divided his clothes among them' (verse 34); 'The people stood watching. And the rulers mocked' (verse 35); 'The soldiers also mocked him' (verse 36); 'One of the criminals having been hanged blasphemed him' (verse 39). At any moment, Jesus could have defended his honour and rebuked these damaged people. But he chose sympathy and silence for them. Only for one did Jesus choose sympathy and speech. One of the criminals asked to be remembered by Jesus in the kingdom of God, to which Jesus replied, 'Truly I say to you, today you will be with me in paradise' (verse 43).

So, in this supreme moment of sympathy, Jesus understands the motivations of those who are hurt. For some, sympathy and silence is the appropriate response. For another, sympathy and speech is appropriate. But, for all, Jesus intercedes to his heavenly Father and seeks mercy and forgiveness for them.

As we develop a sympathetic youth ministry based on a crucified Christology, so we need to pray for wisdom to know when silence or speech might be appropriate. But, at all times, we must never cease praying for those young people to whom we minister – despite the personal sacrifice that this may entail.

Salvation

'Truly I say to you, today you will be with me in paradise.'
(Luke 23.43)

Whatever else the crucifixion was about, it brought salvation. This understanding is at the heart of the Christian faith. It was the foundational understanding of Jesus as he died on the cross. If that were not the case, he would not have been able to turn to the criminal dying next to him and state with such confidence, 'Truly I say to you, today you will be with me in paradise' (Luke 23.43).

Bringing others to salvation, then, must be a central focus for all of us in ministry who want to build on a crucified Christology. The temptation is to subconsciously replace the pursuit of salvation with various forms of social work in ministry. We feel called to Christian youth ministry because we have perceived the need of so many young people among whom we live and work. If we did not perceive the needs of those who hurt, we would be ineffective as ministers. However, in meeting the needs of others, we need to understand that we are actively involving ourselves in a salvation-ministry. Too often, we are led to believe that those who 'preach the gospel' are doing the salvation work and those who 'tend the wounded' are undertaking a lesser social function. This is simply not true. Salvation has a much wider scope than leading people to praying the prayer of commitment so that their eternal destiny is secured. Salvation is about today as well as tomorrow.

In the Western world at least, it is common for the doctrine of salvation to have become an individualized and 'futurized' notion. I am saved. You are saved. I will be saved. You will be saved. Salvation is about me and my God, you and your God. The content of concern about salvation is principally about whether you and I – as individuals – will gain eternal life when we die. The problem with this approach, of course, is that it does not have much to say to a community. Nor, indeed, does it have an impact on the way the world is beyond the transformation of individuals for future benefit. This approach minimizes the impact of the salvation-ministry of Jesus Christ. When we consider that ministry as recorded in the Gospels, we see that his concern for bringing followers to eternal life was not just an event for 'beyond the grave'. Eternal life has a very real impact on the 'here and now' and radically transforms the way in which society operates.

In Luke 4.18–19, we find recorded the words of Jesus' mandate for the kingdom of God:

> 'The Spirit of the Lord is upon me, because of which he anointed me to preach good news to the poor. He has sent me to proclaim liberty to captives and recovery of sight to the blind; to set free the oppressed and to proclaim the year of the Lord's favour.'

In John 10.10, the promise of Jesus to every believer is that we should 'have life – life in all its fullness'. These claims of Christ were designed to encourage neither individualistic piety nor futuristic idealism. These claims were both transformative and present. They represented the ideals of a man who healed the sick, raised the dead, challenged the authorities and transformed the social, religious and political institutions of the day. They proclaimed the vision of a Messiah who would stand with the poor, the vulnerable and the outcast.

That same Christ, that same vision, those same ideals are at the core of our salvation-ministry to young people today. Our task is to introduce young people to that same Jesus who promises the same for us today and from whom they can expect the same liberation. Regardless of social status or economic environment, people need to know the same Christ who can transform their daily living and free them to become the people they were destined to be.

What is needed is a Christology – an image of Christ – that will take seriously a need for individual and personal salvation as well as an ability to transform the structures of society. Since the Christian message is one of liberation, we need to discover afresh a liberation Christology that is creative, vibrant and relevant to young people in the twenty-first century.

There are many theologies of liberation expounded across the globe at the present time: Black Theology, Dalit Theology, Feminist Theology, Womanist Theology, Gay Theology and so on. What all these theologies hold in common is that they are responses to particular communities and have something to say about how Christ brings salvation to their society. Salvation may look different to a coffee-grower in South America than it does to, for example, an oppressed Dalit woman living under the caste system in India or a young black boy living in the Bronx in the United States of America. Inevitably, there is a social and political dimension to salvation for each of these oppressed groups. For them, salvation is as much about how Christ can impact their world today as it is about hope for the after-life. It is a grave mistake, however, to assume that we can just transport the principles of one liberation theology into our own ministry environment. Many have tried to do that and failed. What we need to do, to develop an effective ministry based on a crucified Christology, is to understand what salvation may look like to the particular group we are working with and apply the principles accordingly.

In christological terms, liberation theologies respond to poverty and human degradation by claiming these injustices to be an offence to Christ and an affront to human dignity. A credible Christology – a credible Christ – is dependent upon the degree to which Christians are prepared to address injustice and inequality in society. The challenge, then, is to recognize that Jesus is interested in the circumstances of those to whom we minister who may be oppressed because of their age or the colour of their skin or the earning potential of their parents. As we minister to these young people, there is no point developing a Christology that talks only about the hope of salvation after death. What we need to do is bring Christ to bear on their life circumstances. Injustice is evil. Oppression is evil. Christ will confront sin, evil, poverty, injustice and oppression and a credible salvation-ministry is based on a Christology that emphasizes this.

A few years ago, I had the privilege of working in some Delhi slum districts with a team of youth workers. In that depressed and deprived area, there were two separate projects running. The first was a medical project for young people. Run by a doctor who had sacrificed a promising career to live among the poor, the team provided clean bandages and creams for those who had leprosy as well as giving injections and tablets for the most basic ailments that had become life-threatening in that environment. The second project was run by a charismatic church fellowship, based 15 miles away in a good suburb of Delhi. Every Friday and Saturday evening, a team of young people would come into the slum district, sing worship songs on the streets, hand out Christian tracts to the teenagers and encourage them to come to faith. As darkness fell, they would clamber back into their mini-bus and drive back to their nice houses on the other side of Delhi. They were two very different forms of Christian ministry, both effective in their own way. But we might be right in claiming that Christ was most evident through the work of the doctor and not so much through the charismatic outreach activity. A salvation-ministry founded on a crucified Christology would emphasize this, for three reasons.

First, a crucified Christology is the foundation for human dignity. Human beings – all human beings – have dignity and an innate sense of self-worth. However, the oppressive structures of society often have a dehumanizing effect. Multi-national corporations can dehumanize by paying minimum wages to workers that keep them in poverty. Law enforcement agencies can dehumanize by institutional racism within their ranks. Religious institutions can dehumanize by encouraging literate, educated clergy at the expense of those who struggle with academia. But when the Word became flesh, he gave a renewed sense of dignity to humanity by uniting it with the Divine. Since that event, there is something very precious about human beings purely because God has assumed humanity into his very nature. When Jesus ascended into heaven and returned to the right hand of God, he retained his human nature as well as his divine nature. But in order to achieve that, he had first to be crucified. The message of a crucified Christology is that, united to the crucified Lord, we are special purely because of our humanity.

Second, a crucified Christology is the basis for social transformation. Jesus of Nazareth was a historical figure who brought meaning and salvation to other historical figures. The real Jesus rolled up his sleeves and got on with the real business of getting his hands dirty for God. But our concern in ministry must never be just a historical enquiry through which we bring people into contact with an interesting historical character. Our concern must always be to bring Jesus into a present situation. Jesus of Nazareth is not just some interesting liberator from history. He is the divine presence in the present who can bring liberation to this particular group of people at this particular time. This is achieved primarily through the present reality and power of his message. Jesus Christ is a great prophet, preaching against institutional sin and oppression, defending the poor and warning the rich. Jesus Christ is devoted to the kingdom of God. His whole ministry was – and is – geared up to bringing in that kingdom. But the kingdom of God is not just for the next world. The kingdom of God means salvation in the here and now. The kingdom of God involves the transformation of political and religious structures so that they no longer oppress the individual. Jesus of Nazareth was the founder of a great religious and social movement and he has given us the way to follow in our own ministry. When we undertake that ministry by imitating the crucified Christ, there he is in the midst of us.

Third, a crucified Christology provides a social dimension to salvation. Through his preaching ministry, Jesus enlisted followers to a historical movement that would perpetuate his value-system. It is through that movement – the Church – that salvation can be experienced. If salvation is about being freed to live under the values of the kingdom of God, it is the Jesus movement that becomes the community base to embody that kingdom. Salvation, then, is essentially about living in a community or society that is governed by the principles of the kingdom of God. Within that community, each individual has dignity and a sense of self-worth. Within that community, there is equality of opportunity. Within that community, there is freedom from oppression, inequality and injustice. Defined as such, salvation is essentially about relationship with one's neighbour. Salvation is a social dynamic and a crucified Christology is the bedrock upon which the community is founded. It is the responsibility of all those in Christian ministry to bring young people into the Jesus community. That may or may not be the same thing as bringing young people into your local church.

Surrender

> 'Father, into your hands I entrust my spirit'
> (Luke 23.46)

There is a lovely story told about a vicar who had a young curate come to join him in the parish. For the first few weeks, the curate eagerly watched the vicar as he preached the Sunday morning sermon. For years, it had been the dream of that curate to develop a powerful preaching ministry. It had been his motivation for going into full-time ministry. At times, he had caught himself daydreaming about standing in the pulpit before a huge congregation, hushed in awe at his eloquent words as he expounded the Scriptures for them. More than anything else, he wanted to become known as a preacher of extraordinary renown – a modern day John Wesley!

After a few weeks in the parish, he came to preach his maiden sermon. The curate had spent hours and hours crafting it. He had every word worked out, every physical gesture to be used was noted in the margins. He had studied the commentaries, read the text in the original Greek and developed excellent illustrations with which to illuminate his masterpiece.

Proudly (but with just enough modesty and reverence to look suitably holy), the curate climbed into the pulpit to deliver his sermon. The next 20 minutes were a complete disaster! Everything that could possibly go wrong went wrong. He lost his place on the page, he stumbled over his words and the congregation looked at him with a mixture of puzzlement and uninterest. At last, his ordeal was over. The curate, suitably chastened, walked slowly down the steps of the pulpit with his head held low in genuine humility.

After the service, the vicar sat with him in silence as the curate tried desperately to excuse his poor performance.

Eventually, the curate asked the vicar in exasperation, 'So, tell me, what did I do wrong?'

The vicar looked him in the eye and said quietly, 'If you had gone up into the pulpit the way you came down from the pulpit, then you would have come down from the pulpit the way you went up into the pulpit.'

Think about it!

Those of us called to Christian youth ministry are motivated by a genuine desire to help those in need. In the pursuit of that, we may spend many hours with people or preparing for meetings, Bible studies and so on. Christian youth ministry is not easy for any of us and, often, we grow tired through the demands placed upon us. The temptation is for us to carry on in our own strength, relying on our own abilities and ideas. The simple message of a crucified Christology, however, is that we can only ever minister successfully when we learn to stop trying so hard and start surrendering ourselves to God. We must stop trying to minister out of *chronos* and begin to minister out of *kairos*.

Jesus was absolutely reliant on God the Father throughout his earthly ministry. That reliance and sense of personal surrender did not diminish as he was being crucified. According to Luke, his final words proved that: 'Father, into your hands I entrust my spirit' (Luke 23.46).

This cry of surrender is one of the most beautiful moments in Scripture. After all the physical pain, emotional agony and spiritual doubt, Jesus was still able to trust himself to his Father with real confidence. Quite simply, surrender was the answer to his anxiety.

Christian ministry often makes us anxious. There are so many needs to be met, so much work to be done. In my role as a youth ministry adviser, I once visited a church leadership team who wanted advice on developing their effectiveness with young people. For half an hour, they made a presentation to me about the young people in the community who were not being reached by the church, the social ills and temptations befalling these teenagers and how they were labouring under the guilt of failing in their mission. I asked them to tell me what youth work was currently happening at the church and they listed literally dozens of activities: coffee shop, youth group, choir, Beavers, Cubs, Scouts, Rainbows, Guides, Pathfinders, Explorers, schools work, sailing club and so on. Perplexed, I tried to reconcile the gaping hole they said existed in their youth work with the litany of activities they mentioned.

'So roughly how many young people come through this church in activities each week?' I asked.

'About 500,' they answered before quickly adding, 'but there are so many more in the community that we don't meet.'

While I applauded their desire to extend the mission of the church, I suggested that the first step was to stop feeling anxious and guilty. They should learn to rejoice in bringing the gospel to 500 young people a week! That was an awesome ministry in itself. They looked at me with complete bewilderment, unable to get beyond the self-imposed anxiety and guilt under which so many Christians labour.

There is a huge difference between ministering in the strength of God (*kairos*) and being driven by human anxiety (*chronos*). Those of us in Christian youth ministry need to learn the difference, for the sake of those we work with as well as for our own sanity! We must learn, from the crucified Christ, that absolute surrender to God is required and that his strength can only be truly found in our weakness.

The cost of a crucified Christology

Sorrow, sympathy, salvation and surrender are the hallmarks of a ministry built upon a crucified Christology. Devoting ourselves to that model will inevitably cost us dearly. But personal sacrifice is an unavoidable consequence of modelling our ministry upon the Saviour who was prepared to die so that we may be forgiven. Death, however, was not the only cost to Jesus in modelling a crucified ministry to us. As we mentioned at the beginning of this chapter, Bonhoeffer noted that, 'When Christ calls a man, he bids him come and die.' The death that is required of us need not be physical; there is a death to self, a death to personal ambition, a death to individualism required. In the same way, Jesus undertook a crucified ministry even before the physical act of crucifixion occurred. In winning salvation for us, Jesus made himself completely and utterly vulnerable in a way that cost him dearly. The salvation-ministry of Jesus involved the absolutely unconditional offer of forgiveness. This is a concept we often pay lip service to without really thinking through the personal implications for Jesus.

It is often said that the art of good leadership is never to fight battles that you cannot win. Good leaders, it is said, do not go into a conflict situation unless they are absolutely sure of what the outcome will be. Jesus, however, turned that ideal on its head. Time after time, culminating in his death, Jesus offered forgiveness and acceptance to people without setting prior conditions and without knowing what the outcome would be. Time after time, Jesus accepted the sinner absolutely unconditionally without once looking for a guarantee that the sinner would follow him thereafter. The reality, then and now, is that Jesus always takes the initiative with sinners without first waiting for them to repent. Jesus welcomes the sinner into his presence in the hope that he or she will then repent. A crucified Christology portrays Jesus as a vulnerable Saviour who offers salvation without any preconditions or guarantee that it will be accepted.

Taking that approach to ministry, Jesus makes himself utterly vulnerable because he opens himself to the possibility of rejection. Taking that approach, Jesus is a Saviour so intent on sealing the forgiveness of our sins that he chooses to identify with each one of us at the lowest point of our humanity. Jesus does not relate to us on the level of the best we have to offer. His salvation-ministry is about Jesus touching the very dregs of our humanity. That is where salvation operates in practice; Christ meeting individuals at the lowest and most forsaken point of their being. Jesus forsook the glory of heaven so that he can meet with us as we truly are. That desire took an incredible act of love, compassion and vulnerability on his part.

Jesus offers salvation without any guarantee of a positive result. Ironically, our God is *not* like the father in the story of the Prodigal Son (Luke 15.11–32) who waits anxiously at the top of the road for our return. Our God is a Father who leaves his house, travels down that dangerous road on his own, unsure of where he is heading, and then climbs into the pigsty with us and begs us to come home. Our God is not content to stay in the safety of his own house. He journeys into the very heart of the human tragedy, which is sin.

Salvation is a dirty business for God. There is a tremendous personal cost to him in offering us forgiveness. It is a crucified and crucifying ministry for him. So it is for each one of us who is involved in Christian ministry. It is a dirty business. We must continually make ourselves vulnerable. We must continually open ourselves up to rejection. We must continually reach out to those in need, giving of ourselves with no guarantee of a return. We must continually die to ourselves without ever counting the cost. That is the model to us of a crucified Christ. That is the youth ministry model born out of a crucified Christology.

Yes, it can be a tough, bitter, costly, agonizing ministry. But it is the ministry to which we are called. There is no greater privilege than that.

Pause for thought
- What does it mean for you to die to self?
- How does sorrow for others exhibit itself in your ministry?
- What prevents you from giving yourself totally to others in ministry?
- How do you cope with rejection? How would that differ if you were to develop a crucified model for ministry?
- What scares you most about this model? How might you deal appropriately with that fear?

4

A resurrection ministry

It is not just evangelical bias that claims the resurrection of Jesus as the basis of the ministerial and missionary calling of the Church. It is also the opinion Paul expressed so unequivocally in 1 Corinthians 15.14–19:

> If Christ has not been raised, then our preaching is in vain and also your faith is senseless. Moreover, we are found to be false witnesses about God, because we bore witness about God that he raised the Christ whom he did not raise if then the dead are not raised. For if the dead are not raised, neither has Christ been raised; and if Christ has not been raised, your faith is useless for you are still in your sins. Then those also who have fallen asleep in Christ have perished. If only for this life we have hope in Christ, we are to be pitied more than all men.

If the resurrection of Jesus did not happen, we do not have hope. If we do not have any hope, there is no gospel message out of which we are able to minister effectively to young people.

It is important, then, that we look to the resurrection of Jesus to develop a model of ministry that can impact the lives of young people. At first glance, this appears to be an easy thing to do. After all, do we not, every Easter, celebrate the glorious resurrection of Jesus and rejoice in the hope that this event has given? Do we not proclaim the victory that is ours through the resurrection? Do we not go out into the world in the strength of that victory? Surely the celebration of Easter Day is all we need to know about developing a resurrection ministry. If only it were that simple! There is far more to it if we want to be truly faithful to the christological model of resurrection ministry. Like Christmas, it is sometimes difficult to separate the fact from the fiction of an Easter faith. If we do that, we will be in a better position to develop a ministerial style that takes seriously the reality of the resurrection of Jesus Christ.

Seeing the wood for the trees

As with the nativity and Passion stories, there is an ambiguity between the Easter narratives and message. There is a chasm between how the narratives describe the events and how the message impacted on the Church. With regard to the Easter story, Günther Bornkamm, in his book *Jesus of Nazareth* (1960), deals with this point particularly well.

First, Bornkamm elucidates the sequential differences between the Gospels themselves and the Pauline epistles. For example, Paul mentions that Jesus

> appeared to Cephas, then to the Twelve. Then he appeared to more than five hundred brothers at once, of whom the greater part are still living, though some have fallen asleep. Then he appeared to James, then to all the apostles, and last of all he appeared to me also, as to one untimely born.
>
> (1 Corinthians 15.5–8)

However, there is no mention in the Gospels of Jesus appearing to Peter alone, nor to the 500, nor James. Second, Paul locates most of the appearances of Jesus around the area of Galilee. However, the Gospels (especially Luke) focus the post-resurrection appearances around Jerusalem. Bornkamm argues that the Easter *message* developed before the Easter *stories* were written and the latter echo the former. As he concludes (1960: 183), 'They give empirical expression to the event of the resurrection in individual stories.'

This is an important point for us to notice. The truth is that the Church has developed a ministerial expression based solely on the *message* of the resurrection rather than on the *story* of the resurrection. In one sense, this has enabled the Church to develop a ministerial expression that is full of hope, confidence and claim to victory. That, however, is only half the story. What is needed is to redeem the *story* as well as the message. In so doing, we will develop a far more holistic and richer approach to ministry.

Resurrection: sadness and despair

If we strip away the *message* of the resurrection, what is the most predominant motif? Is it hope? Is it confidence? Is it a claim to victory? Far from it! The *story* of the resurrection is a story of doubt, despair, depression, confusion and pain. As Bornkamm noted:

> One would have to turn all the Easter stories upside down if one wanted to present these people in the words of Faust: 'They are celebrating the resurrection of the Lord, for they themselves are resurrected.' No, they themselves are not resurrected. What they experience is fear and doubt, and what only gradually awakens joy and jubilation in their hearts is just this: They, the disciples, on this Easter day, are the ones marked out by death, but the crucified and buried one is alive. Those who have survived him are the dead, and the dead one is living. (1960: 184–5)

The Gospel resurrection story is one in which the disciples are left in utter confusion. They hide away fearfully (John 20.19), they refuse to believe that Jesus has been raised (Luke 24.11), and they return to the fisherman lifestyle (John 21.3).

How far removed all this is from the *message* of the resurrection! In the *story*, the resurrection creates nothing more than dismay, fear, denial, cowardice, scepticism and rejection. Bizarrely, in the *story*, the resurrection seems to be bad news!

The *story* of the resurrection is clear. The resurrection is not, foremost, about our victory in Christ. The resurrection, foremost, is about human weakness as well as divine victory. The resurrection is about our complete defeat in the light of Christ's complete victory. Since that is the case, the first thing we must acknowledge, if we want to develop a truly christological youth ministry founded on the resurrection, is that we are weak and defeated and our ministry must reflect that.

This is good news for ministry because it allows us to develop an empathetic approach. The last thing that young people need, when they are in pain or confused or burnt out by life, is to have someone sit with them who has all the answers! Empathetic ministry demands a different approach. Empathy demands that we assume a position of weakness and vulnerability; to hurt with the hurt, to cry with those who are in despair and to mirror back to them something of the frailty of human existence. How can we do that if we are coming from a position of victory, confidence and joy?

It is far better, far more empathetic, to minister alongside the hurting from a position of genuine fragility and brokenness. That is what Henri Nouwen meant by the title of his book, *The Wounded Healer* (1979). We are called to be wounded healers as Christ was the wounded healer for us. Ironically, it is only when we recognize the power of the resurrection that we can become confident enough to assume such a vulnerable position. It is only when we know what it is to be utterly defeated that we can sit with those who feel defeated in their own lives. Human despair, as a vital component of the resurrection story, makes that possible.

That being the case, it is true to say that *kairos*-ministry is itself, in part, an experience of brokenness and frailty. This should not surprise us in the light of our previous chapter, of course. *Kairos* involves a death to self; it is, in part, a process of unbecoming in order to become. Particularly in the early days of developing the spiritual discipline, it can be a fearful thing to consciously step out of *chronos*-activity and into *kairos*-awareness. All of our usual safeguards are removed and those aspects of the ego-state that bolster our sense of 'self' are dismantled. When we are ministering to broken young people, it is far more comfortable to do so in *chronos* because that protects us from being confronted by our own vulnerability. But a resurrection ministry demands that we have the courage to move into *kairos*, despite the vulnerability we experience.

It has been a deep privilege through my years of ordained ministry to sit with many people as they have died. I do not think there is any deeper honour than to share that moment of intimacy with someone. I will never forget my first such experience. A teenager called Peter was dying of cancer. I had sat with him for many hours over the previous few weeks as his condition deteriorated and I held him in my arms as he died. Most of the time, we had sat in silence. I was silent as he finally passed away. For many months afterwards, I chastised myself for not having said something profound to him at the end. I hated myself for not bringing a verse of Scripture to him or a promise from God. It was a long time before I forgave myself and finally realized that all Peter really wanted was to be held and loved during his final moment on earth. Unwittingly, I had offered him a *kairos*-moment at death rather than try to fill 'the time' with words, which would have been an ego response (*chronos*) on my part, determined to play the role of 'competent priest'.

Resurrection: joy and confidence

It is only as the story develops and the disciples (and the early Church community) are able to reflect on the *message* contained within that attitudes change and develop. Then the implications of the resurrection become clear; death is defeated, sin is overcome, our resurrection is secure in him, the prophecies have been fulfilled in Christ and he is eternally alive. Once this message has been realized, joy and confidence begin to replace sadness and despair.

Despite what we have considered above, it would be a weak ministerial position indeed that embraces only despair, fragility and confusion. If a man is drowning, there is no point jumping into the river to drown with him! We would only jump in, embracing the fragility of his situation, if we felt that there was a possibility of leading him out of danger. For that reason, the resurrection message encourages us to minister through confidence too. The only way in which we can understand the power at work within us is by a comparison with Jesus' resurrection. However, as David Prior rightly notes,

> Perhaps the resurrection and ascension of Jesus do not indicate transcendence so much as displacement and replacement: a whole new world has been generated – its character and qualities were sketched out in the life and death of Jesus; its reality has burst into our existence in the resurrection and ascension of Jesus. In particular, the Holy Spirit brings substantial and increasing glimpses of this new world, as he goes to work in Christian believers to produce the very life of Jesus in our mortal bodies. For this to happen, the old must be displaced and replaced with the new. (1988: 159)

This is an incredible claim – an incredible reality. The truth is that the same power is at work within each one of us as was used to raise Jesus from the dead! There is no other power we could possibly need to be effective in Christian ministry. We have, quite literally, all the power in the universe at our disposal! But note that it is God's power, not our own; any power we may have had must become displaced if we are to become effective ministers. Since this is the case, there is no room for personal triumphalism. Modelling ourselves on the incarnate ministry of Jesus, we can experience the power of a resurrection ministry when we learn to give of ourselves and deny ourselves. As Prior states, 'This self-denying, self-giving lifestyle contains within it the power of God' (1988: 160).

God says that, 'My power is perfected in weakness' (2 Corinthians 12.9). This must have been a hard lesson for Paul who, throughout his life, had known what it meant to have power and privilege as an educated Roman citizen from a fine family, known and respected for his spiritual zeal and sharp mind. For Paul to become weak in order to have God's power perfected in him for ministry must have been a painful journey of self-discovery. The same is true for each one of us. However, it is only when we learn to embrace weakness and vulnerability that we can gain confidence and hope in ministry. Ironically, both vulnerability and confidence are two sides to the resurrection coin. We cannot have one without the other.

A story to think about

Jesus addresses the issue of resurrection as a concept in his debate with the Sadducees, recorded in Luke 20.27–38. The importance of this interaction for our purposes, however, is that this was no mere academic debate. As well as its acting as some sort of precursor to his own resurrection a few days later, Jesus also provides us with important insights into the resurrection life that can have a profound impact on our youth ministry methodologies.

The Sadducees have become well known to us for their denial of the resurrection. The reason for their denial was their theological conservatism; that which was not taught in the Torah must be treated with suspicion. To be sure, some of the later prophets taught a resurrection doctrine – Ezekiel and Daniel, for example – but the earliest Jewish books did not. To the Sadducees, these were the ultimate authorities. In order to show the stupidity of the resurrection doctrine, the Sadducees attempted to catch Jesus out by offering a seemingly absurd example.

> Now there were seven brothers; and the first having taken a wife died without a child; and the second and the third took her, and likewise the seven did not leave children and died. Lastly, the woman also died. Therefore, at the resurrection, whose wife will the woman be? For seven were married to her.
>
> (Luke 20.29–33)

However, the story is not as absurd as it may at first seem. In fact, it is rooted in the Torah, Deuteronomy 25, in which the law states that the brother of a deceased man must marry his widow if there were no children born of that first union. Such a law was perfectly reasonable in a society in which procreation, and therefore the protection of property for generations to come, was deemed to be a dominant purpose for marriage. Indeed, the story of Ruth gives us insight into the pragmatic outworking of this law.

At the heart of this interaction between Jesus and the Sadducees is the question about the nature of the resurrection life. The response of Jesus is very illuminating.

First, Jesus is clear that resurrection life is very different from pre-resurrection experience:

> The sons of this age marry and are given in marriage. But those who are considered worthy of taking part in that age and in the resurrection from the dead neither marry nor are given in marriage. Indeed, neither can they die any more; for they are angels and are sons of God, being sons of the resurrection.
>
> (Luke 20.34–36)

There is clearly a radical discontinuity between the two modes of existence. Death no longer has any dominion in the resurrection life. This discontinuity impacts every aspect of existence, including our relationships (marital partners, relations with our children and so on). Second, in a brilliant piece of rhetorical genius, Jesus draws the Sadducees back to their precious Scriptures, the Torah, to prove that God is God of the living, not the dead: 'That the dead are raised, even Moses showed on the bush, when he calls the Lord the God of Abraham and the God of Isaac and the God of Jacob. For he is not God of the dead but of the living, for all live to him' (verses 37–38). This passage from Exodus 3, re-interpreted by Jesus, clearly indicated that there is no limit to the Fatherhood of God. Indeed, the family of God is not delineated along racial lines but according to faith. Paul made this clear in his letter to the Romans where he commented that,

> because of this faith it is that, according to grace, the promise to all of the seed, not to that of the law only, but also to that of the faith of Abraham, who is the father of us all. As it has been written: 'I have made you a father of many nations.'
>
> (Romans 4.16–17)

Through a stroke of ingenuity, Jesus had used the Sadducees' own weapon to disprove their thesis. The Torah clearly reveals the eternal love of God that cannot be extinguished by death. Those who are in the faith will be raised to new life.

Jesus knew that he was provoking dangerous consternation by undermining the authority of the Sadducees. They were, after all, in league with the Romans in the ruling of Judea; the religious elite who controlled the masses through spirituality as the Romans controlled them through law and societal discipline. But in so doing, Jesus was getting to the heart of the truth about resurrection. This incredible act of God was not only counter-natural but counter-cultural too. The Sadducees represented the spiritually privileged of Israel – those who were to be honoured and respected by God and man alike. However, the challenge of Jesus was that it is not they who shall be honoured for all eternity but the common man who exercises faith. Resurrection is open to all who believe, regardless of social and religious status. Resurrection is the ultimate democratization of religious experience. Resurrection is the gateway to a new world order under the lordship of Jesus Christ. Resurrection is nothing short of an exodus moment. It is therefore not surprising that, in speaking of resurrection, Jesus draws on a passage related to the great exodus event. The other great resurrection story in the Old Testament – the valley of dry bones in Ezekiel 37 – is also set in the context of an exodus; this time the return from exile in Babylon. Through the death and resurrection of Jesus, which makes our own resurrection a possibility, an exodus from the old world order into the new world order becomes a reality.

It is no coincidence that Luke locates this debate with the Sadducees in the context of chapter 20. The whole chapter is devoted to stories about people attempting to catch Jesus out. In verses 1–2, the chief priests and the teachers of the law enquire of him, 'Tell us by what authority you are doing these things.' In verse 19, we are told that, 'The teachers of the law and the chief priests looked for a way to arrest him immediately, because they knew that he had spoken this parable against them.' In verse 20, we are told that the same teachers of the law, 'Keeping a close watch on him . . . sent spies, who pretended to be honest'. Throughout this chapter, Jesus is called upon to justify his ministry and spiritual authority. What greater way to prove that authority than by alluding to the power of resurrection!

A resurrection ministry

In terms of developing a christological youth ministry, we need to reflect on what this passage has to tell us of the resurrection life that can be experienced this side of the grave. Interpreted as such, we can see that this story offers enormous hope for those to whom we minister in the light of the resurrection. New life in Christ is such an important possibility for those who are hurt and desperate for healing. But personal renewal is only part of the story in the light of this passage from Luke 20. Given the challenge that Jesus presents to the Sadducees, the spiritual powerbrokers of his day, there is a deeper, perhaps more profound, element for us to consider. The new world order which is ushered in by the event of resurrection is a direct challenge to the political systems and institutions that hold many in bondage in our contemporary society. Implementing a resurrection ministry that is truly christological in emphasis necessarily involves challenging injustice; it is the eradication of poverty, it is concern for the created order, it is the writing-off of crippling Global South debt so that the dying may live, it is the toleration and embracing of racial and religious diversity, it is the promotion of gender equality, it is the development of love and respect for the Other – whoever they may be. Resurrection, as well as a personal spiritual experience, is an ethical transformation that operates on a societal level. If we are to develop a truly christological ministry, we cannot ignore our responsibility to work towards an ethical resurrection of our communities, both local and global. As Paul noted in his letter to the Romans,

> the eager expectation of the creation awaits the revealing of the sons of God. For to futility the creation was subjected, not willingly, but through the one having subjected it, in hope that the creation itself will be freed from the slavery of decay into the freedom of the glory of the children of God.
>
> (Romans 8.19–21)

What is this but a great proclamation of the power of resurrection operating on a cosmic level? A christological ministry, that takes resurrection seriously, will work towards the realization of that.

The gift of *kairos* in resurrection care

We know from our ministries that the resurrection of Jesus is the ultimate stumbling block for many who would otherwise wish to profess faith. It is hard enough to comprehend the resurrection as a *chronos*-event. How much harder to be intellectually reconciled to it as a *kairos*-event! That is to say, it is hard for anyone, on a rational level, to discover eternal value and meaning in an event that is barely comprehensible even as a historical act.

The resurrection, as a *kairos*-event, is counter-intuitive. For those who are suffering or bereaved or grieving, it is not easy to make sense of Paul's statement, 'Death has been swallowed up in victory' (1 Corinthians 15.54). How are we to walk purposefully with young people in their experience of death in a way that offers hope? The answer cannot be purely a presentation of the resurrection of Jesus as a *chronos*-event. Those who grieve are not looking for one more fact to believe. They are desperately seeking a transformative experience. To be effective in ministry, we must ourselves comprehend resurrection as a *kairos*-event.

Young people, as with all of us, need to know that there is something stronger than death. The experience of *chronos* is the experience of the finite, the failing and the passing. *Chronos*-time contains within it the very being of death. *Chronos*-time ebbs and flows away, taking with it all that is impermanent and subject to change and decay. Pastoral ministry will involve us in helping young people be reconciled to the bitterness of *chronos*-time, the inevitability of loss contained within *chronos*-time, the pain of life and death that so defines *chronos*-time. But as we seek to gently lead young people through the journey of loss, we want them to experience the truth of resurrection as a *kairos*-event.

If the experience of *kairos* is the experience of eternal value in relationship to the Other, we know that there is no greater eternal value than love (1 Corinthians 13.13). We are convinced, then, that love infuses *kairos*, and is the ultimate value of *kairos*-ministry. Since Christ's resurrection is such a profoundly important *kairos*-moment, it was – and is – infused with love, for us and for the whole of creation. Therefore, we can confidently claim that love itself is stronger than death. Love overcomes the deepest moments of separation. Love is an infinite *kairos*-experience that redeems and ultimately transcends the finitude of *chronos*.

That being the case, when we offer pastoral care to young people, we are not only seeking merely to help them or alleviate their pain, which addresses just the *chronos*-problem. Ultimately, we are seeking to lead them into an experience of the actualization of love. To love a young person who hurts is a *kairos*-based resurrection ministry at its most profound level. If we try only to help and alleviate pain in pastoral ministry, we will be left frustrated because there is often little we can do to achieve those ends. But there is nothing that can frustrate love, as Paul reminds us in Romans 8.38–39:

> For I am persuaded that neither death nor life, nor angels, nor rulers, nor things present, nor things to come, nor powers, nor height, nor depth, nor any other created thing, will be able to separate us from the love of God in Christ Jesus our Lord.

Here is the irony. Help is not stronger than death. Only love is stronger than death. But as we seek to love those in pain, we give them the true help they need. We cannot rescue young people from their pain. But as they experience your *kairos*-focused resurrection ministry, they will encounter the rescue of God in and through you.

Love is the greatest pastoral gift you have to offer. Love is the ultimate gift of resurrection. Love is the ultimate *kairos*-value. As John reminds us,

> God is love, and those who remain in love remain in God and God remains in them . . . There is no fear in love, but perfect love casts out fear . . . and this is the commandment we have from him, that whoever loves God must love his brother also.
>
> (1 John 4.16, 18, 21)

Pause for thought

- What does it mean for you to be a 'wounded healer'?
- How might you be able to use vulnerability and frailty in your own ministry to support others?
- What should you be celebrating with young people in your local community? How can you encourage your church to celebrate with you?
- What does love look like in your pastoral encounters? How can you move away from the priority of 'help' to the priority of 'love' in your ministry?

5

An ascended ministry

The Ascension of Christ is perhaps the most neglected and misunderstood aspect of Christology. How many books about the Ascension do you have on your bookshelves? When was the last time you heard a sermon on the Ascension and its practical application for our lives? When did you last refer to the Ascension in your own teaching of others? If these questions are making you squirm with a slight sense of embarrassment, then welcome to the club! Other than on Ascension Day, we hear very little indeed of this most important aspect of Jesus' life. When it is spoken of theologically, it is more often than not subsumed into the joy and victory of the resurrection. When it is spoken of historically, it is more often than not passed over as the narrative moment when Jesus said 'Goodbye' to the disciples and left them to get on with the work. The Ascension of Jesus is treated as little more than the 'happy ending' of his time on earth; a nice story that clears the way for Pentecost.

The Ascension, however, is far more than that. The Ascension is nothing less than the pivotal moment of the New Testament narrative; the ending of the Jesus-event in history and the beginning of the story of the Spirit-filled people of God, the Church. As we shall see, we would have no pneumatology, no ecclesiology and certainly no eschatology to speak of were it not for this momentous ascension experience. We would certainly have no personal experience of *kairos* breaking into *chronos*; were it not for the Ascension that experience would remain unique to the incarnate Christ alone. In short, the Ascension, perhaps more so than the resurrection, is the pivotal moment of salvation-history for it is through the Ascension that we are finally brought into the presence of God; the moment that *chronos* becomes inhabited by *kairos* for the whole of the created order.

It is Luke, of course, who relates to us the account of the Ascension of Jesus – not once, but twice (Luke 24.50–53 and Acts 1.6–11). While some have tried to make hay with the 'discrepancies' between his two accounts, it is clear that this Gospel writer recognized the importance of the event itself: for Luke, as we have just mentioned, it was a 'conclusion' to the earthly ministry of Jesus and a 'beginning' to the epoch of the Spirit. It is therefore natural that he should wish to present it both at the end of his Gospel and at the outset of his account of the early Church. Whatever difference between details of the story itself may be inferred, the theological message is constant.

Additionally, many have claimed that the Ascension should be viewed as a fictional event. In *The Message of Acts*, John Stott cites William Neil as agreeing with Harnack (among others) by declaring that, 'It would be a grave misunderstanding of Luke's mind and purpose to regard his account of the Ascension of Christ as other than symbolic and poetic' (1990: 47). However, as we shall come on to see, any denial of the historicity of the Ascension not only weakens the Christian message but irrevocably collapses the gospel imperative and all missiological endeavours. Quite simply, the historical Ascension of Jesus Christ is absolutely essential to effective Christian youth ministry.

Through the act of ascension, Jesus has returned to the Father, from whence he came. He had earlier assured his disciples that such a return would be necessary for their own good:

> Do not let your heart be troubled. Believe in God, and believe in me. In my Father's house are many rooms; if it were not so, would I have told you that I go to prepare a place for you? And if I go and prepare a place for you, I will come again and will take you to myself, so that where I am, there you may be also.
> (John 14.1–3)

This, of course, was difficult for the disciples to understand. Thomas replied, 'Lord, we do not know where you are going. How can we know the way?' Jesus' response, 'I *am* the way . . .', is most instructive. It is only in relationship with him, and in seeing *his* journey as *our* journey, that we can come to the Father. As Jesus had to go via the cross, resurrection and Ascension, so we too must take the same route to God. Paul fully understood the implications of this:

> Do you not know that as many as were baptized into Christ Jesus were baptized into his death? Therefore we were buried with him by baptism into death, so that, as Christ was raised from among the dead by the glory of the Father, so we also should walk in newness of life. For if we have become united in the likeness of his death, we will also be united with him in the resurrection.   (Romans 6.3–5)

In his excellent (and definitive) book, *Ascension and Ecclesia*, Douglas Farrow states that, 'Jesus' ascension, considered as a priestly act, begins already on the cross; or rather his whole life is seen as an act of self-offering that culminates in the cross. In the ascension this offering is received on high' (1999: 34). If, as Paul suggests, we are united with Christ in death and resurrection, we are most certainly united with him in ascension also. The importance of this truth for youth ministry will become clear as this chapter unfolds.

The Ascension and time

During my years as an Anglican parish priest, I have officiated at literally hundreds of funerals. As bizarre as it may sound, it has always been my favourite part of the job. What an immense privilege it is to share with a family at perhaps the most vulnerable and painful moment of their life. How wonderful it is to have people take me into their confidence and share their deepest sorrows. I count it a real joy to do what I can to bring comfort and share the gospel with them as and when appropriate. When I was first ordained, I asked a soon-to-be-retiring vicar if he had any advice for my ministry. He thought for a few moments and said, 'Perform every funeral as if you were burying your own mother.' I never forgot that advice and take great care in the preparation of funeral services. Like most clergy, I often inter-weave poetry into the funeral liturgy. Some poems are unique to that occasion but, more often than not, the family request one that means a great deal to them that they had heard else-where or read in an anthology. One of the most popular in this regard is the poem 'Gone from my Sight' by Henry Van Dyke:

> I am standing upon the seashore. A ship, at my side, spreads her white sails to the moving breeze and starts for the blue ocean. She is an object of beauty and strength. I stand and watch her until, at length, she hangs like a speck of white cloud just where the sea and sky come to mingle with each other.
>
> Then, someone at my side says, 'There, she is gone.'
>
> Gone where?
>
> Gone from my sight. That is all. She is just as large in mast, hull and spar as she was when she left my side. And, she is just as able to bear her load of living freight to her destined port.
>
> Her diminished size is in me – not in her. And, just at the moment when someone says, 'There, she is gone', there are other eyes watching her coming, and other voices ready to take up the glad shout, 'Here she comes!'
>
> And that is dying . . .

The comfort that this passage brings, of course, is that there are two 'perspectives' on the death of someone we love. The first, most immediate perspective, is that of those who are left behind crying, 'There, she is gone!' The second perspective, however, is that of those who stand on the other side, those who are watching for the arrival of the deceased, who take up the glad shout, 'Here she comes!' The comfort of this passage is that our response to death is a matter of perspective, a matter of sight, dependent upon which shore we are standing on.

The Ascension of Jesus is no different. There are two perspectives on this event recorded in Scripture. In Acts 1.9, we read of the disciples standing on one shore: 'And having said these things, he was taken up from their sight, and a cloud hid him from their eyes.' Luke, however, was not the first biblical writer to narrate the ascension event. Incredibly, we need to go back to Daniel 7.13–14 for that. In this Old Testament passage, we read of the same event, this time, though, narrated from 'the other shore':

> I saw in the night a vision, and behold with the clouds of heaven, one coming as a son of man, and he came to the ancient of days and was brought near to him. And to him was given the authority and the honour and the kingdom and all the people, tribes and tongues will serve him; his authority, an eternal authority, will never pass away, and his kingdom shall not be destroyed.

The Ascension is an event-in-time (a *chronos*-event) that can be viewed from two perspectives, both the 'going' and the 'coming'. Both of these perspectives are provided in Scripture with the Lukan account giving realization to the fulfilment of the prophetic writings from centuries before. The Lukan account has the disciples saying, 'He is gone!' The Daniel account has the hosts of heaven saying, 'Here he comes!' It is for this reason that the Ascension has a profound impact on how we, as Christians, consider the notion of 'time' and its impact on our ministry to others.

We have realized already that how we perceive the notion of 'time' is a complex issue, of course. However, to serve our present purposes, we note that Jesus Christ entered *chronos*-time through his incarnation and, through his Ascension, now exists outside of *chronos*-time in *kairos*-time. That is not to say, though, that Christ has nothing more to do with us. In the light of Paul's comments in Romans 6, which we looked at earlier, we are united with Christ through his death, resurrection and Ascension. There is a sense in which we, like Christ, exist both within *chronos*-time and outside of *chronos*-time. We are united with him in *kairos*-experience that can break into our *chronos*-experience.

This may seem, at first glance, as nothing more than an abstract and obscure philosophical notion. However, there is an important impact on our ministry through this; namely, how we approach pastoral difficulties with our young people. It is hard for all of us to get a sense of perspective on the difficulties that life throws up at us. How much more so is that true for young people! Breaking up with a boyfriend, not having the 'right' clothes to wear for a party, falling out with a best friend, not being picked for the school football team – these can all seem like catastrophic moments for a teenager! (I remember struggling to remain sympathetic with a 17-year-old girl in my youth group as she sat sobbing uncontrollably because her father had bought her a second-hand Ford for her birthday and she had wanted a brand-new Peugeot: 'My friends will think I am *such a loser.*') Some crises they face might indeed be very painful; the death of a sibling, family breakdown through divorce, diagnosis of a serious illness and so on. The challenge for us, as we minister to these young people in pain, is not to provide answers so much as to give a perspective on their situation through which they can know the presence of God with them.

Viewed from the perspective of space and *chronos*-time, pastoral difficulties may seem insurmountable and, sometimes literally, soul-destroying. Immersed in the moment of pain, there may seem to be no escape. However, viewed from an eternal perspective, from the perspective of *kairos*-time, there is always hope. This is not to say that there is ever an excuse for trite responses to pastoral problems; comments like 'God must have a reason for it' and 'You just need to trust that God has it all planned out' are pastorally inappropriate and never justified. Rather, the eternal *kairos*-perspective – the truth that the young person is united with Christ and therefore beloved by God – has the potential to bring about a sense of security, even in the midst of temporal, *chronos*-insecurity. Jesus' 'present' is glorification in God, since he has now ascended to the right hand of God the Father. His 'present' is not only our 'future hope' but also the possibility for our 'present' too, if we choose for this to be our current perspective. Just as Luke records the 'going' of Jesus and his 'coming' is recorded in Daniel, just as the ship 'goes' from our shore and 'comes' to another shore in Henry Van Dyke's poem, so there is a choice of perspective on our present experience. We can choose a perspective that focuses on loss and pain (*chronos*) or we can choose a perspective that has as its focus the love and compassion and glory of God (*kairos*).

It is not easy to change our perspective. Far less easy is it for us to minister to young people in such a way that we open up for them new horizons and new ways to approach their own difficulties. However, the Ascension of Jesus, as a present reality, contains within it the possibility of God for today, for this moment. The Ascension of Jesus is the doorway to *kairos*-experience. It is for this reason that the Ascension of Jesus provides a strong foundation for hope; a ministerial gift which is essential for all of us seeking to work effectively with young people.

But here is the contentious issue. The foundation for Christian hope resides in the *Ascension* of Christ and not, as some writers on incarnational youth ministry erroneously suggest, in the *continuing presence* of Christ. We need to explore this in more detail.

The absent Christ

The presence of Christ with us is, for many theologians, at the heart of Christian theology. The presence of Christ with us is, for many Christians, at the heart of their faith. The presence of Christ with us is, for many youth ministers, at the heart of their practice and teaching. It is an idea that brings comfort and support, most especially in the difficult times of life. Therefore, to make the bald claim that 'Christ is not really with you' would shake the very foundations of faith for many people to whom we minister. However, if we are to take the Ascension seriously, we must wrestle with the reality that the Christ who was historically present on earth 2000 years ago is now historically absent. The truth is that Jesus of Nazareth is not here. He has gone elsewhere.

The question that we must take most seriously in the light of the Ascension is simply this: 'In what *sense* is Christ present with us if he is no longer here?' This is no mere theological nicety. The omnipresence of Jesus is a given for most Christians, which is hardly surprising in the light of our discipleship methodologies. Christ with us, Christ in the world, Christ around us – this is often the basis for pastoral comfort instilled in the hearts of new believers. Do we not encourage young Christians to pray to Jesus? Do we not anthropomorphize God in such a way that Jesus is portrayed as an ever-present friend? Does our hymnody not teach this very idea?

The difficulty with this approach, however, is that the historical particularity of Jesus of Nazareth is lost through this doctrine. As Farrow notes, 'Christ everywhere really means Jesus of Nazareth nowhere' (1999: 12). Put most simply, if we believe that Christ is everywhere, we must necessarily de-personalize him. No longer can he exist as the person, Jesus of Nazareth. Instead, we commute his being into pure Spirit, existing in all places at all times. This notion of a continuing presence of Christ takes us beyond the boundaries of orthodox Christian belief. A doctrine of the Ascension that 'de-personalizes' Jesus results in the very same Gnostic dualism against which Irenaeus and the saints of the early Church fought so bravely. Later still, Calvin recognized the importance of this understanding in his *Institutes* (chapter 17, para. 27):

When [Jesus] is carried aloft into the air, and the interposing cloud shows that he is no more to be sought on earth, we safely infer that his dwelling now is in the heavens, as Paul also asserts, bidding us to look for him from thence (Phil 3:20).

No, Christ cannot be omnipresent if we are to remain true to the particularity of Jesus.

It seems, at first glance, that the notion of an absent Christ will result in a hope-less gospel. Perhaps we may feel abandoned by God. Perhaps we may no longer be able to make sense of Jesus' promise to us in Matthew 28, 'I am with you all the days until the completion of the age.' For those of us in youth ministry, we may even feel that one of our greatest 'tools' has been taken away; so much of what we do and what we teach is dependent on a Christ who is 'present'. Without the presence of Jesus, we may feel bereft of a positive gospel message. Nothing, however, could be further from the truth! In reality, it is only the doctrine of an absent Christ that can truly bring any hope at all. This is for three reasons, which we will explore in more detail now.

Ascension and the Holy Spirit

While we are theologically convinced that Christ is absent from the world, and must necessarily be for there to be any sense of Christian hope, we do not want to lose the link between Christ and world. Loss of that link has two major implications. First, it would be *God himself* who becomes absent, not just Christ. Second, the relationship between history (*chronos*) and eternity (*kairos*) would be obliterated. Somehow, it is vital that we retain a 'present God' – even though there is an 'absent Christ' – for there to be any meaning and purpose in the Ascension at all.

That link between creator and created, between history and eternity, is maintained through the Holy Spirit. We may go as far as to say that it is only an 'absent Christ through ascension' who gives meaning to our need for, and the activity of, the Holy Spirit. After all, if Christ were still present, what need would we have for the Holy Spirit?

This is not the book for us to go into great detail about the doctrine of the Holy Spirit – what we call pneumatology – but suffice to say that it is through the Holy Spirit that we are in relationship with God. As Farrow rightly comments, 'Christ's ultimate mission . . . was to draw the Spirit into man and man into the Spirit, that man might truly become a living being' (1999: 60).

In a chapter of a previous book, *God of the Valley*, I have written about the intrinsic worth of each and every human being: 'Actually, you are an OK person' (2003: 82–91). I do not want to cover the same ground here. However, it is important from a ministerial perspective to recognize that human dignity and worth is, in a real sense, linked to the Ascension of Jesus Christ. The writer to the Hebrews makes this link for us by the manner in which he portrays the Ascension as the controlling motif of the salvation-event. Jesus, as priest and king, has sat down at the right hand of God. It is in the light of this 'sitting down' that we can make sense of our own identity.

Jesus has taken our humanity up to God and been found acceptable in his sight. Because of that, our humanity is, by definition, acceptable to God. The link between the broken world and God is re-created through the Ascension because humanity becomes part of the Godhead. It was Athanasius, in *On the Incarnation* (54) who wrote, 'He, indeed, assumed humanity that we might become God.' Likewise, in Homily XI, *Homilies on the First Epistle of St Paul to Timothy*, John Chrysostom wrote, 'For God became Man, and Man became God'; and Irenaeus, in the Preface to Book Five, *Against Heresies*, wrote of, 'the Word of God, our Lord Jesus Christ, who did, through his transcendent love, become what we are, that he might bring us to be even what he is himself'. This notion of *theosis*, properly understood, does not suggest that we become

God in nature and essence but that we become gods through the sharing of Christ's characteristics by communion and conjunction. In the eternal realm, that communion and conjunction is expressed through the dual nature of Christ – divinity and humanity – brought together in the Godhead. In the temporal realm, it is expressed through participation in the Spirit of Christ, which Jesus gifted to us prior to the Ascension.

So it is then, that, through the act of ascension, and the sending of the Spirit, which necessarily preceded that event to prevent an absence of God occurring through the absence of Christ, Jesus re-unites what had become separate through the fall. Heaven and earth become one once more. That is not to suggest an essential coherence (for example, I cannot rightfully claim to be God) but a unity through diversity. Even after the Ascension, Jesus remains both God and man. As the Athanasian Creed reminds us, '[Jesus], although He is God and man, yet He is not two, but one Christ. One, not by conversion of the Godhead into flesh, but by taking of that manhood into God.' And yet the Chalcedonian Definition reminds us that Jesus is,

> Lord, Only-begotten, recognized in two natures, without confusion, without change, without division, without separation; the distinction of natures being in no way annulled by the union, but rather the characteristics of each nature being preserved and coming together to form one person and subsistence, not as parted or separated into two persons, but one and the same.

It is through the Ascension that human beings are given ultimate dignity. Through the Ascension, humanity becomes both assumed into the Godhead (a *kairos*-existence) and bearer of the Holy Spirit (a *chronos*-activity). For an effective youth ministry, it is essential to locate human dignity and worth in this place. This is true because of the theological difficulties we face by trying to locate human dignity and worth elsewhere. An example is the habit of most youth workers to theologically express human dignity and worth as being a result of a young person being a child of God. More often than not, a youth worker will say that 'We are all children of God.' However, Packer contends that this is not necessarily the case:

> You sum up the whole of the New Testament teaching in a single phrase, if you speak of it as a revelation of the Fatherhood of the holy Creator. In the same way, you sum up the whole of New Testament religion if you describe it as the knowledge of God as one's holy Father. If you want to judge how well a person understands Christianity, find out how much he makes of the thought of being God's child, and having God as his Father. If this is not the thought that prompts and controls his worship and prayers and his whole outlook on life, it means that he does not understand Christianity very well at all. For everything that Christ taught, everything that makes the New Testament new, and better than the Old, everything that is distinctly Christian as opposed to merely Jewish, is summed up in the knowledge of the Fatherhood of God. 'Father' is the Christian name for God. (1973: 224)

By implication, not everyone is a child of God; only those who are Christians can lay claim to that relationship. Therefore, if we locate human dignity and worth in the Father/child relationship, we infer that only young people who are Christians have any sense of worth and should be treated with dignity. Of course, we do not want to take that approach! *All* young people, regardless of gender, ability, creed or ethnicity, should be treated with dignity and respect. The common denominator they all share is not necessarily their relationship with God. Rather, it is the fact that their humanity has been assumed into the Godhead and that they are Spirit-bearers.

Because the Ascension of Christ – the absence of Jesus – gives way to a ministry of the Spirit, eternity and temporality – *kairos* and *chronos* – can co-exist. It is for this reason that young people can be empowered and enabled to become the people they were created to be. Kant explored this idea in *Religion within the Limits of Reason Alone*:

It is our universal duty as men to elevate ourselves to this ideal of moral perfection, that is, to this archetype of the moral disposition in all its purity – and for this the idea itself, which reason presents to us for our zealous emulation, can give us power. But just because we are not the authors of this idea, and because it has established itself in man without our comprehending how human nature could have been capable of receiving it, it is more appropriate to say that this archetype has come down to us from heaven and has assumed our humanity.

(Kant, cited by Farrow, 1999: 170)

Essentially, Kant calls for an ascension of the mind that will result in our becoming fully human.

It is exactly this movement towards which so much youth ministry is aimed. Empowerment of the individual, equality of opportunity, informal education and voluntary participation – the four core values of youth work recognized in the United Kingdom – all have as their motivation an inherent 'ascension' towards the achievement of potential. Young people, in the power of the Holy Spirit, are in the process of becoming. Youth ministry is geared towards enabling that process. However, it would be impossible for that to happen without an ascended – absent and Spirit-sending – Christ.

Ascension and the Church

The one thing we do *not* need in the twenty-first century is an ecclesiology that is stuck in the past. Not that the past is unimportant – far from it! One of the prevailing sins of postmodern society is its belief that 'all things are new' and that we have nothing to learn from the past. The negative ramifications of this attitude are huge, on an individual, local and global level. Perhaps more than ever, we *need* the past. However, learning lessons from the past is not the same thing as being stuck in the past. Neither do we need an ecclesiology that is focused too much on the future. Not that the future is unimportant – far from it! In the next chapter, we shall be examining just how important eschatology is for the purposeful development of a Christlike ministry. The ecclesiology that is most desperately needed in the twenty-first century is an ecclesiology that gives meaning to the *present*, with one eye on the *past* and one eye on the *future*. If the Christian faith does not give meaning to the present, it is worthless. Meaning for the present is what we all crave, is what our societies must experience if we are to experience any sense of peace. Whatever else our own Christian ministries bring, they must surely seek to bring meaning for today into the lives of those who have no sense of meaning for it is in this realization of present meaning that Christology, pneumatology and ecclesiology all come together. If we believe that the Church has something to offer in the search for present meaning, we must take the Ascension seriously because it is the act of ascension – the establishment of the reign of Christ at the right hand of God – that makes Pentecost and the coming of the Spirit to his people possible. The stark truth is that the Church is founded on the Ascension.

The problem seems to be, however, that in discarding the historical particularity of the post-Ascension Jesus in a desire to create a doctrine of a Christ who is continually present, the Church has become confused as to the nature of the Lord she confesses and preaches. Historically, the Church has always struggled to comprehend the humanity of Christ. That is not surprising, given the way in which the Ascension has been treated through the years. There are just two examples I wish to explore in regard to the impact of this on youth ministry.

First, the Ascension makes sense of the sacraments, most especially the eucharistic meal, and encourages us to see this as an effective tool for working with young people.

We know that there has been much debate since the Reformation as to the presence of Christ – or otherwise – within the eucharistic elements. For Ulrich Zwingli, the Ascension was proof enough of the bodily absence in the elements. Luther took an approach that embraced omnipresence but did not endorse transubstantiation. In his own inimitable style, expressed in *Against the Fanatics*, he commented:

> Listen now, you pig, dog, or fanatic, whatever kind of unreasonable ass you are: Even if Christ's body is everywhere, you do not therefore immediately eat or drink or touch him; nor do I talk with you about such things in this manner, either; go back to your pigpen and your filth . . . the right hand of God is everywhere, but at the same time nowhere and uncircumscribed, above and apart from all creatures.
>
> (Luther 1526, cited in Placher 1988)

However, what is known as Luther's Ubiquity Notion (Christ everywhere at once) again dehumanizes Christ in its attempt to present omnipresence. Calvin, perhaps more than any other Reformer, grappled with the question of an absent Christ. He firmly understood the need for an absent Christ, even in the sacrament itself, otherwise, as he wrote in *Institutes* (chapter 17, para. 33), 'no slight insult is offered to the Spirit if we refuse to believe that it is by his incomprehensible agency that we communicate in the body and blood of Christ'.

But if Christ is not 'present' in the sacraments because he has ascended, in what sense can we be united with him through the eucharistic meal? One may argue that Christ does not 'come down' to us in the sacraments. Rather, through participating in the Holy Spirit, we are 'lifted up' to him as we receive bread and wine. In a ritualistic Kantian sense, we ascend to heaven by participating in communion; heaven does not come down to us. *Chronos*-time and space is transcended through an act of the Spirit, not through a barbarization of Christology through the denial of ascension. As Farrow comments, 'The ascended Lord is not everywhere . . . but he *is* everywhere accessible' (1999: 178). It is through the Holy Spirit that we access the glory of heaven in the act of the Eucharist.

That being the case, we can use the Eucharist as a particularly powerful tool in youth ministry. This is increasingly the case, especially in the re-discovery of the power of ritual and symbolism so prevalent, particularly, in the New Monastic movement.

Second, the Ascension strengthens the need for mission to young people. We have seen that, through this act, the link between the fallen world and God is forged and healed. It therefore becomes essential that the young people we are ministering to are introduced into that relationship so they can fulfil their destiny. Since the eucharistic community ascends to God, it would be true to say that the Ascension happens *in us* rather than (or as well as) *to us*. This relocates the Church as a community of meaning. It is essential that young people are brought into the body of Christ so that they can participate in that. Only in the Church can young people truly come into relationship with God. It is a place of destiny. This is not an argument for any particular 'form' of Church or denomination – it is a theological statement. Indeed, it may be that we need to abandon some traditional forms of Church – and allow our existing denominations to die – because they are no longer living out that destiny and are therefore becoming increasingly irrelevant for effective youth ministry.

Because of its eucharistic nature, the Church must be an 'ascending community': always moving in a dynamic fashion towards the ascended Christ in the power of the Spirit. In Romans 12.2, Paul wrote, 'Do not mould yourselves to this age, but be transformed by the renewing of the mind, so that you may approve what is the will of God – the good and pleasing and perfect.' Paul Tillich, in *The Eternal Now*, commented compellingly on this Pauline imperative:

> Many churchmen would perhaps agree with this. But they would resist, if one applied the warning of the apostle to the church itself. But we must do so ... For the Christian churches also belong to this aeon ... They share in the corruption of this

aeon, its mixture of good and evil . . . I do not hesitate to state that one may have to resist being conformed even in the church community. Certainly, such an act also involves a risk. One may be in error. But it must be done . . . Here we see what non-conformity ultimately is – the resistance to idolatry, to making ultimates of ourselves and our world, our civilization and our church. And this resistance is the most difficult thing demanded of a man . . . It is almost too difficult for human beings. It is not too difficult to become a critic and rebel. But it is hard not to be conformed to anything, not even to oneself, and to pronounce the divine judgment against idolatry, not so much because the courageous act may lead to suffering and martyrdom, but because of the risk of failure. It is hard because something in our conscience, a feeling of guilt, tries to prevent us from becoming non-conformist.   (1963: 122–3)

What the Ascension proves is that, in terms of ecclesiology, historical *chronos*-acts can contain within them the essence of *kairos*-eternity. A sacramental community that is prepared to operate in the power of the Spirit and the truth of an absent Christ for the furtherance of its mission is proof of that fact. This must form the basis of a Christlike ministry that understands the message of the Ascension.

Ascension and the second coming

Finally, we note that the Ascension has ramifications for eschatology too. I do not propose to say much about this since the next chapter is dedicated to the impact of eschatology on Christian youth ministry. However, it is important to recognize the obvious truth that, without the Ascension, there would be no second coming. Quite simply, if Christ had not left, he would not be able to return!

Traditional paintings of the Ascension almost always portray Jesus disappearing into the clouds with adoring disciples looking up as his body is assumed into a cloudy sky. The Copernican revolution, which followed considerably later than his death

to that understanding from a cosmological
...emingly not from an emotional one. A philo-
...ination of Acts 1.11 was necessary: 'Men of
...ou stand looking toward heaven? This Jesus,
...ken from you into heaven, will come in the
same way as you saw him go into heaven.' The establishment
of an anticipated new world order was now to be considered
teleological rather than literal. Calvin, in *Tracts* 2/286, wrote,

> When Scripture speaks of the ascension of Christ, it declares,
> at the same time, that he will come again. If he now occupies
> the whole world in respect of his body, what else was his
> ascension, and what will his descent be, but a fallacious and
> empty show?   (Calvin, cited by Farrow 1999: 176)

The glory of the absent Christ

The Church exists in a period of the absence of Christ. This is
not to be denied or ignored; in a sense, it is to be celebrated. In
Ascension and Ecclesia, Farrow lays down a powerful challenge
to the Church:

> If even the Church will not acknowledge the absence of Jesus, how
> can the world hope to learn of it? How can it hope to have its
> attention drawn now, before the parousia and the day of wrath,
> to him whose intercession with the Father does not preclude
> but requires that he come also as judge?   (1999: 272)

The absent Christ of the Ascension is no empty doctrine or
theological wordplay. It is a reality that lies at the very heart of
our missionary imperative. We are tasked, in youth ministry,
to prepare those to whom we minister for the second coming
of Jesus in judgement upon the whole of creation. How can we
prepare them for that coming if we act as if he is still here?
How can we lead them into a healing experience of the Holy
Spirit, the gift of God to us, if we proclaim a 'present Christ'?
We may be able to present a more cosy image of God, a more

friendly, brotherly image of God, through speaking of a Jesus who is always with them, no matter what. But we do so at a tremendous cost. The Holy Spirit is prevented from playing as full a role as he might in their experience of discipleship. The Trinity, therefore, becomes little more than an abstract doctrine – certainly not a present, personal and powerful experience of dynamic love. Ultimately, if we teach a 'continually present Christ', we rob our young people of hope since the return of Christ is that upon which all hope is founded.

Ultimately, if we deny the historical fact of the Ascension and thereby teach a 'continually present Christ', we deny the very ministry we strive to achieve.

Pause for thought

- What have you taught young people about the Ascension to date?
- To what extent do you teach young people about a 'continually present Christ'? Would you reassess this in the light of what you have read?
- What emotions does the notion of an 'absent Christ' throw up in you?
- How might you use the sacrament of Holy Communion to instil a sense of dignity in the young people you serve?
- What does it mean for you to build a culture of dignity and respect for the individual in your ministry? How might the Ascension help you to do that?
- In what ways might you be able to focus more on the second coming of Jesus if you have a more rounded understanding of the 'absent' and ascended Christ?

6

An eschatological ministry

There is undoubtedly a movement of the Spirit afoot to create missiological communities of faith that are learning to speak powerfully into our postmodern context. Within mainstream denominations, we celebrate the Fresh Expressions movement. Outside of mainstream denominations, we look towards the New Monastic movement and the Emerging Church movement to see the Spirit at work in new ways. As Christendom continues to face the challenges of massive societal changes, so new ways of doing Church continue to emerge. It is an exciting period of Church history!

However, the question continues to be asked – and is nowhere near fully answered yet – as to which of the 'old bricks' of a modernity-shaped faith can be successfully re-used in the building of the new viable Christian world-view and, by implication, a viable Christian methodology for youth ministry. It would be contrary to God's character to dispose of all the old bricks and use only new ones. (He did, after all, re-use even Noah and two of each type of animal after the flood!) Part of our task in today's Church, particularly for those of us involved in youth ministry, is to scavenge what we can from the collapsed temple of Christendom that may be of use in building the new. It is a dirty job. We will get covered in dust. We will cut our hands and bruise our feet. We will need imagination to see how an old piece of masonry may look beautiful in a new mosaic. But the hard task will be worth the effort.

The argument of this chapter is that eschatology is one of those bricks worth salvaging and polishing for effective Christlike youth ministry. To be sure, it needs cleaning up and will need some careful cementing. Nevertheless, with care and attention, I believe that christological eschatology can once more look beautiful and will have a pivotal role to play in the missiological task that faces the Church among young people in the twenty-first century.

A hitchhiker's guide to christological eschatology

The word 'eschatology' is a mid nineteenth-century word, meaning 'talk about the last things' or 'discourse on the last things'. As such, eschatology is the context of all our thought about God. Everything we do as Christians, everything we think as Christians, is done and thought in the context that, one day, Christ will return and this world will be wrapped up for good (however you may choose to interpret that). We are heading towards a new heaven and a new earth and everything else should be placed in that context. Indeed, it was Karl Barth who commented, 'If Christianity be not altogether thoroughgoing eschatology, there remains in it no relationship whatever with Christ' (1968: 314). The ultimate question of eschatology is simply this: 'How does God relate past, present and future to us now?' Just as pertinently, how are we to relate to God in the light of the past, present and future? Eschatology, essentially, is about the history of the world. It deals with the realities of today's world, which are working together to bring about God's future. Eschatology is the big picture, if you like, the ultimate fusion of *chronos* and *kairos*.

Traditionally, there have been two main divisions in eschatology; general eschatology and individual eschatology. General eschatology deals with those issues that have to do with the wider picture: creation, the consummation of the kingdom, the nature and purpose of the second coming of Christ and so on. Individual eschatology deals with those issues of a more personal and individual nature: physical death, the nature of the soul, judgement and so on. It is a biblical theme that has roots in both the Old Testament and the New Testament, both aspects of which are intimately linked to the person of Jesus Christ.

Admittedly, there is not a huge amount of teaching on the type of eschatological themes mentioned above in the Old Testament. But that is not to say that the Old Testament does not have a lot of eschatological teaching. There are six key themes to unpack.

The expectation of a coming Redeemer

From Genesis 3.16 onward, there is the expectation that the Redeemer will eventually come: 'I will put enmity between you and the woman, and between your seed and her seed; he shall bruise your head, and you shall bruise his heel.' This, of course, is an eschatological idea; the idea of a cosmic battle between the forces of darkness and the Redeemer.

The kingdom of God

The term 'kingdom of God' is not actually used in the Old Testament but there are many, many references to God as king. Because Israel is so lost in sin, the story of the Old Testament is one in which God's rule is only imperfectly realized. The prophets look forward to the day when the kingly rule of God will be fully consummated, which is an eschatological theme. The book of Daniel is the main book where the coming of God's kingdom is outlined most. In chapter 2, there is mention of God's kingdom that will be set up and will never be destroyed and which will break into pieces all other kingdoms. Again, in chapter 7, there is the idea of the Son of Man who will be given everlasting dominion and power. So, in Daniel, we see a linking together of these two eschatological ideas: the coming Redeemer and the kingdom of God.

The new covenant

The idea of covenant – the fact that we live in a covenant rela-tionship with God – is a central idea in the Old Testament. In fact, it's the idea on which Old Testament theology is built. Because Israel constantly broke its covenant obligations, there was the need for a new covenant and this is an eschatological idea which we find, for instance, in Jeremiah 31.31–32:

> See, the days are coming, says the Lord, when I will make a new covenant with the house of Israel and the house of Judah, not like the covenant which I made with their ancestors when I took them by the hand to bring them out of the land of Egypt, my covenant which they broke.

Of course, that new covenant is ushered in by Jesus and becomes fully realized at the second coming.

The restoration of Israel

The nation of Israel was divided into two kingdoms: Israel and Judah. These two kingdoms sank into disobedience and Israel was scattered and Judah was taken into exile. Again, it is Jeremiah who predicted the restoration of Israel (23.3): 'I will gather in the remnant of my flock from all the earth where I have driven them, and I will place them into their pasture, and they shall increase and multiply.' Isaiah and Ezekiel and, not least, Joel who prophesies the outpouring of the Spirit as a sign of the restoration of the people Israel, echo this view: 'And I will give portents in the heavens and on the earth, blood and fire and columns of smoke. The sun shall be turned to darkness, and the moon to blood, before the great and terrible day of the Lord comes.'

The Day of the Lord

This is a complex idea in the Old Testament. Sometimes, the Day of the Lord refers to God's judgement on Israel's enemies (Obadiah, for example, speaks of the judgement of Edom as being the Day of the Lord) but it can have an eschatological aspect too. For example, we read in Isaiah 13.9–11 about God's judgement on Babylon. However, it is also written in eschatological language that conveys a deeper meaning:

> Behold, the day of the Lord comes,
>> cruel, with wrath and fierce anger,
> to make the world a desolation
>> and to destroy its sinners from out of it.
> For the stars of heaven, and Orion, and all the host of
>> heaven
>> will not give their light;
> and it shall be dark at sunrise
>> and the moon will not give her light.
> I will punish the world for its evil,
>> and the wicked for their iniquity.

The new heaven and the new earth

Isaiah 65.17 states, 'For there shall be a new heaven and a new earth; and they shall not remember the former things nor shall they be in their hearts.'

The pattern of Old Testament eschatology is clear. From the garden of Eden, there were eschatological expectations and, as time went by, these expectations became more highly developed and more diverse and complex in their various forms. But certainly, eschatology is an important aspect of Old Testament literature.

Likewise, eschatology is an important theme in the New Testament too. There are three threads in particular to draw out.

The Old Testament eschatological event has happened

The Christ-event was the fulfilment of literally hundreds of Old Testament prophecies. In Matthew, Jesus' birth was prophesied in the Old Testament and so was his flight into Egypt, his triumphal entry into Jerusalem and his being betrayed for 30 pieces of silver. There are many other prophecies we could draw on from the Old Testament which were fulfilled in Jesus' life and death, proving that there is a clear understanding in the New Testament that this eschatological kingdom, which was anticipated in the Old Testament, was ushered in by Jesus Christ and that Jesus Christ was the eschatological Messiah and the eschatological Son of Man. Because the eschatological event has happened in Jesus, the New Testament writers were absolutely convinced that they were living in the last days. So Peter, on the day of Pentecost, quotes from Joel's prophecy and Paul, particularly in his early Epistles, was convinced that Jesus was about to return at any time.

The realization that eschatology is a twofold movement

The eschatological event had come to pass in Christ but the New Testament writers were also clear that the first coming of Christ was just the first part of the twofold eschatological movement. The present messianic age would be finally consummated in the age to come.

The blessings of the present age are the guarantee of greater blessings to come

The first coming of Christ is the guarantee and pledge of his second coming, Acts 1.11: 'Men of Galilee, why do you stand looking into heaven? This Jesus, who was taken up from you into heaven, will come in the same way as you saw him go into heaven.' The eschatological promise for the future is rooted in what has happened in the past. Christ won the victory in the past on the cross and the future consummation of the kingdom of God and all the blessings we will receive as kingdom children is founded on that victory. The reason we have so much hope for the future is not because we have so little now but because we have so much now: so many riches, so much grace, so much mercy.

Making the links

So what does all this have to do with ministry and mission among young people in today's society? Is there anything that we can learn from the biblical data that will provide guiding principles for us in the twenty-first century? My belief is that the biblical data does indeed provide the core principles for a contextual missiology that takes eschatology seriously, for this reason: our contemporary culture is an age of tension and ontic anxiety and biblical eschatology speaks into that in such a way as to provide a platform for relevant missiological praxis.

Paul Tillich, in *The Courage to Be*, explored this in some depth, noting three forms of anxiety in particular, all of which 'are immanent in each other but normally under the dominance of one of them' (1952: 50). First, there is what Tillich called 'ontic anxiety', a preoccupation with death. Second, there is anxiety about personal guilt and anxiety. Third, there is a spiritual anxiety of emptiness and loss of meaning.

The twenty-first century is one in which we live with heightened levels of anxiety. The threat of global terror, ecological disaster, work-related stress, dysfunctional families, civil wars, increasing levels of violence in society, financial worries caused by increasing levels of debt are signs of the times. The threat of death and the feeling of personal guilt are compounded by a deep societal sense of emptiness and loss of meaning. Reflecting on the Church's response – or lack of response – Douglas John Hall is right to pose the question, 'Why have we Christians failed to produce soteriologies that speak to the anxiety of our age in the way that Anselm and the Reformers spoke to theirs?' (2000: 410). His critique is that the Church is hesitant to enter into the anxiety that shapes our societies, that the Church is somehow paralysed and thereby prevented from speaking into the spirit of the age.

There may be truth in that. Arguably, the witness of the Church in the face of ontic anxiety is to make generalized statements that affirm a certain doctrinal position at best, ambiguity at worst: God stands with the poor, God condemns social injustice, we are to be stewards of creation, the breakdown of the nuclear family is to be lamented and so on. The prayers in our churches often reflect that generalized approach, with priest and laity alike fearful of praying 'the wrong thing' that may cause offence, not so much to God, but to their fellow worshippers. So we pray for 'wisdom for our leaders' but we pass by the opportunity to name before God the specifics of their political wrongdoings. We ask for a 'spirit of generosity' rather than actually proactively giving of our own money to the poor in our communities. We intercede for 'peace in war-torn regions of the world' rather than acknowledging our responsibilities to protest and campaign and hold our political masters accountable for their indifference.

Ontic anxiety will never be relieved by generalizations. Ontic anxiety will only ever be dispelled by pragmatic, culturally specific and localized responses. As Tillich concluded, 'The contents of the tradition, however excellent, however praised, however loved once, lose their power to give content *to-day*' (1952: 55).

It is this agenda, to meet the ontic anxiety of the age through pragmatic, culturally specific and localized action, that should drive the Church in the twenty-first century. This is particularly pertinent to our study in the light of Tillich's conclusion that, 'It is significant that the three main periods of anxiety each appear at the end of an era' (1952: 68). Why should this be the case? Quite simply, states Tillich, because 'Conflicts between the old, which tries to maintain itself often with new means, and the new, which deprives the old of its intrinsic power, produce anxiety in all directions' (1952: 68). Clearly, a new missiology is required. A christological missiology that takes seriously the ontic anxiety of the age through eschatological contextualization can offer that.

The simple fact is that eschatology is to do with ontic tension. This is necessarily the case, almost by definition, since Christian eschatology is founded on the paradox that (a) The kingdom of God has already come in Jesus and (b) The kingdom of God has not yet come. There is a tension between the *chronos*-event of the incarnation and the consummation of *kairos*-experience that lies in the future. Christian youth ministry is most often about helping young people to come to terms with – and live peaceably within – that paradox. It is the context for a missiology that speaks powerfully into the human situation.

There are all sorts of tensions into which the gospel speaks: tension in our spiritual life (Romans 7.18, 19, 25b); tensions in our use of time (2 Peter 3.8; Philippians 4.5); tensions in our use of wealth (1 Timothy 4.4; Luke 16.13); tensions between suffering and glory (Acts 14.22; 1 Peter 4.12, 13); tensions between sickness and health (Matthew 11.4, 5; 2 Corinthians 12.7); tensions between faith and doubt (1 Corinthians 13.12) and so on. Increasingly, in a society driven by ontic anxiety, the task of the Church will be to embody a ministry and mission focused on the Christ who brings healing to those who live with the paradox of those tensions. The message, increasingly, will need to be a message of hope; not that the tensions will be eradicated but that there can be peace and wholeness – and, crucially, hope – in the midst of ontic anxiety rather than through the eradication of it.

Towards a 'hopeful' eschatological ministry

In the light of the ministerial endeavour that faces the Church, those of us involved in youth ministry need to rediscover the prophetic teaching of Jürgen Moltmann on the theology of hope. Perhaps more than ever, his teachings should be embraced and applied. Moltmann, the German prisoner of war whose personal experience of ontic anxiety led him to write the brilliant 1964 *Theology of Hope*, was concerned to relate the biblical teaching on eschatology to the experience of human beings living in a time of rapid social change. Half a century later, his words are of profound importance to our era and, crucially, speak into the experiences of so many young people.

The genius of Moltmann has been to really ground eschatology (and therefore hope) in the person and work of Jesus Christ. He wrote:

Christian eschatology does not speak of a future as such ...
Christian eschatology speaks of Jesus Christ and *his* future ...
Hence the question whether all statements about the future are
grounded in the person and history of Jesus Christ provides it with
a touchstone by which to distinguish the spirit of eschatology
from that of utopia.   (1964: 17, italics original)

The Christ-event, the first coming of Jesus, is absolutely crucial
for eschatology and, for Moltmann, the resurrection is the pivotal
point. The resurrection is the bridge between the hope of Jewish
prophecy and apocalyptic writings on the one hand and the
eschatological mission of the Church on the other. It is the
resurrection that provides the content of hope to the experience
of the people of Israel. It is the resurrection that provides the
content of hope for the Church and its mission in these last days.
For Moltmann, Christian eschatology is based on the history
of God's promises and their fulfilment.

The story of Scripture, the story of the Church since Scripture – perhaps our own story, even – is that God's promise does
not correspond to reality as we know it. God's promises and
the hope he offers often contradict our perception of reality.
In our world-view, we see guilt and anger and hostility and
confusion. For many of us, suffering and guilt and death are
our experience of the world. But the promise of hope to us,
made through the resurrection, is that, actually, God's reality
is very different and the glories of the kingdom of God are
there for all through Christ. But the very fact that there is a
qualitative difference between our present experience and the
'theology of hope' that God offers puts Moltmann's ideas into
the eschatological realm. By experiential definition, there is
something 'now' but 'not yet' about the hope of the Christian
faith. There is always the possibility for us to return to despair,
doubt and temptation because we are living in that unresolved
period of ontic anxiety. However, there is also the possibility for
us to cling on to the divine promise: 'The expected future does
not have to develop within the framework of the possibilities

inherent in the present, but arises from that which is possible to the God of promise' (1964: 103).

Because he has an eschatological context, Moltmann says that of course it is impossible to fully know God in this present age. As Paul writes in 2 Corinthians 5.7, we are walking by faith and not by sight. In the language of Moltmann, we are living in a promise for the future and it is in the future that all things will be revealed: 'All proofs of God are at bottom anticipations of that eschatological reality in which God is revealed in all things to all' (1964: 281). So eschatology is something to be worked towards, not something we can fully claim for the here and now. Of course, this has tremendous ramifications for ministry. There are, for example, new horizons of possibility for believers; there is hope for the future based on a solid historical reality. We are freed to become missionary people working for the renewal of the world. It is also true, for example, that all things become possible in Christ; institutions can be transformed, societies can be changed and injustice can be challenged. In a wonderful quote, Moltmann assures us that 'Faith can expend itself in the pain of love, and assume the form of a servant because it is upheld by the assurance of hope in the resurrection of the dead' (1964: 338).

An apologetic for eschatology in a postmodern era

You may well ask the question why it is that the creation of a christological eschatology is needed at all in a postmodern era. Has eschatology not been one of the most controlling meta-narratives the Church has used to oppress throughout history? Is there any way of developing a christological eschatology that liberates rather than oppresses? My argument is that there is – and Moltmann's theology of hope points the way forward.

The most powerful purpose of eschatological theology in the last 30 years or so is the way in which it has stimulated social action and social responsibility. A Christian Marxist called Nicholas Lash stated that, because of eschatology, religion is not the opium of the people. Rather, it is the stimulant of the people (1984: 161). Certainly the existentialist philosopher Søren Kierkegaard glimpsed that too with his much cited phrase, 'Hope is passion for the possible.' However, I think Christian hope is more than that in its eschatological sense. Hope is not so much passion for the possible. Hope is passion for the promised.

What is most exciting for the Church agenda is that this 'promised' is not just individual but communitarian too. Hope, in this postmodern, connected world in which we live, is not just an individualistic concept. Hope is for all of God's creation too. Creation spiritualities – and iconic spiritualities, too – have a strong eschatological content as well as context. But more important still, when we consider the nature of hope, is that modern eschatology has demanded a rewriting of the doctrine of God. Moltmann's emphasis on the future promise has been taken up, by some, as a doctrine of God not as one 'who is' but a doctrine of God as one 'who will be'. So, for some theologians, like Schillebeeckx, God as a future promise is more important than the idea of God in the here and now. That doctrine of God helps suffering communities and the marginalized have a renewed sense of hope when they cannot find God in their present context. Most important of all in this regard are the writings of Karl Rahner who says that God is first of all God of the future rather than a God of the present. In *A Theology of Liberation*, Gutiérrez comments that, 'The liberating action of Christ – made man in this history . . . – is at the heart of the historical current of humanity; the struggle for a just society is in its own right very much part of salvation history' (1973: 168).

For too many years, the Church has allowed eschatology to be hijacked by theologians and institutions that have oppressive political agendas. In its passion and desire for a new contextual missiology that speaks into the ontic anxiety of the present age, the Church must be careful not to throw the baby out with the bathwater. Eschatology need not be oppressive. A christological eschatology that has hope at its very heart could be immensely liberating, both for individuals and communities. Ultimately, spiritual liberation – both for individuals and communities – is the mandate of the Church.

Eschatological youth ministry

I have had the privilege of being involved in youth ministry around the world for some decades now. I have had the privilege of training hundreds of youth workers and listened to their stories of ministry. In the midst of all that diversity, there is one constant: young people are looking for hope. Hope is only found when life takes on meaning. Meaning is only achieved when *chronos* is inhabited by *kairos*.

Ultimately, the focus of an eschatological youth ministry is the nurture of young people so that they can experience the profundity of *kairos* in their mundane *chronos*-existence. For some, that will be a profoundly spiritual encounter; perhaps coming to faith in Jesus Christ and finding new purpose in life through that new relationship. For others, it may not be named as a spiritual experience at all; perhaps the restoration of a broken relationship with a parent, perhaps finding a sense of purpose in a new job or training opportunity, perhaps a growing realization of what it means to be a responsible member of society. All of these are examples of how *kairos*-meaning can be experienced in the mundanity of *chronos*-time. All of these examples are, to some extent, eschatological in that they are the breaking in of the eternal into the present. We know that these are eschatological moments because they are moments that produce hope and, as Paul reminds us, hope is an eternal (and therefore eschatological) quality: 'And now remain faith, hope, and love, these three things' (1 Corinthians 13.13).

This should serve as a real encouragement to all of us involved in youth ministry. Often, we feel discouraged that so much of our time is spent on mundane matters. Perhaps we long for more opportunities to share Christ with young people. Perhaps we secretly disdain the amount of effort we must put into supporting young people through the ordinary aspects of their lives; studying for exams, sorting out yet another relationship breakdown, job hunting, going to court with a troubled young person to act as a character witness and so on. Yet it is in these ordinary activities that young people experience hope for a better future. By walking with them through these activities, we are giving them hope and so engaging in a truly eschatological youth ministry. There is no higher calling than this.

Pause for thought

- What are the most common tensions that your young people experience? How can you help them to gain a fresh perspective on those tensions?
- What does ontic anxiety look like in your local community? How can your church better address the pain of that community-anxiety?
- Where do you see hope rising in your local community?
- What examples from your own encounters with young people can be viewed as the breaking in of *kairos*-hope into the mundane of their *chronos*-living?
- Kierkegaard said that, 'Hope is passion for the possible.' How might that notion shape your youth work curriculum in the future?

7

Jesus: kingdom and discipleship

In our final chapter, we are putting all our thoughts on the development of a christological youth ministry into its appropriate context – that of the kingdom of God. In Mark 1.15, we find the first words of Jesus' public ministry; words in which he sets out his agenda: 'The time [*kairos*] has been fulfilled and the Kingdom of God has drawn near; repent and believe in the Good News.' By now, we should be able to recognize that this is an incredible statement of *kairos* breaking into *chronos*. In that statement, there is a twofold agenda unveiled. First, that the kingdom of God is near; there is a *kairos*-experience to be encountered. Second, that he calls us to repent and believe; there is a *chronos*-activity to be undertaken in order for that encounter to become possible. In this chapter, we will unpack these two ideas and see how they relate to the Christian notion of discipleship.

The kingdom of God

The basic theological meaning of the idea of the kingdom of God was that a new age would replace the old age. The rule of God (*kairos*) would smash apart the old ways of the world (*chronos*) and the kingdom would break through in most dramatic fashion.

But Jesus had an absolutely unprecedented understanding of this concept. The way Jesus understood it was that the future rule of God was, in some sense, present right now – even as he spoke. David Bosch, the extraordinary South African missiologist, commented that, 'Christ has cleft the future in two, and part of it is already present' (1980: 24). As far as Jesus was concerned, the kingdom of God was, in some sense, the presence of the future. The kingdom of God still had to be consummated but it was a present reality. There is, then, a twofold aspect to Jesus' understanding of the kingdom: it is 'now' but 'not yet'; *kairos* inhabits *chronos*. To comprehend this, we must think through this idea of the 'now but not yet' in a little more detail.

First, the kingdom of God is 'now'. Jesus taught that in a real, tangible sense, the kingdom of God was already here. A revolution had taken place and Jesus was here to initiate and announce that revolution. And it *was* a revolution: we must not underestimate the shocking power of Jesus' words. Here was a carpenter from backwater Nazareth coming into the heart of the political and religious establishment, threatening the power of the political and spiritual leaders. He was announcing a new kingdom, a new rule, and, according to Luke 4, Jesus announced that work in the synagogue and said that he would be the revolutionary leader.

Think about the impact of this happening:

> And [Jesus] came to Nazareth where he was raised and he entered, according to his custom on the Sabbath day, into the synagogue and stood up to read . . . 'The Spirit of the Lord is on me because of which he anointed me to preach good news to the poor, to proclaim deliverance to captives, and recovery of sight to the blind, to send out the oppressed in deliverance, to proclaim the year of the Lord's favour.' And having rolled the scroll, having delivered it to the attendant, he sat down; and all the eyes in the synagogue were fixed on him. He began to say to them, 'Today this scripture is fulfilled, in your hearing.'
>
> (Luke 4.16–21)

What an extraordinary challenge to the political and religious leaders of the day!

And it is important that we grasp this: the kingdom of God, as Jesus understood it, was about the rule of God over *all things*.

It was not just a matter of the heart. It was not just about a spiritual internal change. The kingdom of God was a real tangible rule that would impact every aspect of creation. It was a spiritual kingdom, yes, but it also had an impact on the nature of religious institutions, political institutions, the role of slaves in society, the role of women and children, Gentiles and Samaritans and so much more.

We must not just spiritualize the kingdom of God. As Jesus understood it, the kingdom of God was intensely political and very, very tangible. The biblical scholar Joachim Jeremias has rightly commented that,

> Neither in Judaism nor elsewhere in the New Testament do we find that the reign of God is something indwelling in men, to be found, say, in the heart; such a spiritualistic understanding is ruled out both for Jesus and for the early Christian tradition.
>
> (1972: 101)

So, when we see Jesus begin to minister throughout the region of Galilee, we see an intensely tangible ministry revealing what the kingdom of God is all about. The sick were healed; the possessed were exorcized; the dead were raised to life; the hungry were fed; there was authority exercised over nature; spiritual and political leaders were challenged.

But how, specifically, was the kingdom of God a present reality? In five ways:

The kingdom was present in the unique person of Jesus

The kingdom of God was not just something that Jesus announced. In a very real sense, Jesus *was* the kingdom. Jesus was not just the messenger; he was the message too. Jesus was both medium and message. The incarnation was the perfect embodiment of *kairos* within *chronos*.

The kingdom of God was integrally bound up with the person and ministry of Jesus and it still is, of course. Jesus is Lord and the rule of God is exercised over creation through his reign. And because the kingdom of God is located in Jesus, that is what gives so much power to the idea of discipleship. When Jesus, in Mark 1.17 said, 'Follow me', it was, and is, a radically different concept from discipleship to any other religious leader. Because Jesus was not just a teacher or a rabbi, to follow Jesus means to seek and submit to the rule of the kingdom of God.

The kingdom was present in the unique power of God

The Greek word for kingdom is *basileia* (βαςιλεια) and that means 'reign' not 'realm'. The important distinction here is that the idea of the kingdom of God is not a passive thing: it is not to do with a geographical area. The kingdom of God is a pro-active idea: it is a dynamic power, a ministry. It is about effective activity. It is about the 'act of ruling'. In the light of all that has gone before, we might even say that the kingdom is an eternal quality.

The idea of the kingdom of God, in Jesus' understanding, is a pro-active dynamic principle. It is about God's rule invading and breaking through the old age and the old way of living. It is about the kingdom of God in the very person and ministry of Jesus; proclaiming the new way of being and accompanying that proclamation with demonstrations of the power and reality of that kingdom.

The kingdom was present through a new ethical approach

The kingdom of God has a value-system in-built into it. The kingdom of God is an upside-down kingdom. The kingdom of God provides a very real challenge to the values of the world. In the kingdom of God, sinners are welcomed; the outcasts are welcomed. Prostitutes and tax collectors are the friends of God. The ethics of the kingdom of God, as understood by Jesus, challenge the ethics of Judaism and the political authorities. The first shall be last and the last shall be exalted.

The kingdom was present in the poor

It is absolutely undeniable that the poor had, and still have, a special place in the kingdom of God. God is on the side of the poor – and the rich, he shall send empty away. In a very real sense, Jesus was a liberation theologian. His was a political theology of liberation whereby the poor are empowered and in which we are encouraged to see Jesus in the face of the poor.

The kingdom was present by creating a community

We will move on to the community of disciples in a few moments but, at this stage, it is sufficient to note that the creation of a community was one of the greatest signs of the power of the kingdom. The proclamation of the kingdom resulted in the growth of a kingdom community. The story of the Acts of the Apostles is a story of how that kingdom community continued to grow, often in opposition to the religious and political establishment.

So primarily in these five ways, we see that Jesus believed the kingdom of God, in one sense, to be already present and in their midst. The kingdom of God was 'now'.

However, there was also a sense in which the kingdom of God was 'not yet'. When he was talking about the kingdom of God, Jesus also used future language as well as present language. It was here but it was not yet consummated; the work of the kingdom was not yet fulfilled. What is interesting about the now and the not yet is that what was still to come was slightly different from what was already happening.

The kingdom of God has two primary aspects to it. The first aspect is grace and, in the first coming of Jesus – in his Palestinian ministry – Jesus exhibited that grace in all that he did and said. He preached a message of grace. Grace was received through his healing touch. Grace was received whenever anyone encountered him. Of course, ultimate grace was proved through his death on the cross; winning forgiveness of sins for all who would believe in him. So, in the ministry of Jesus, there is a sense in which the 'now' of the kingdom was a 'now' of grace.

Kingdom grace became real through Jesus Christ. The 'not yet', though, holds a different kingdom dimension: God's judgement. Jesus warns of judgement and he spoke of it often. However, that judgement will only become a cosmic reality at the second coming of Christ: the day of visitation. Judgement Day.

The 'now' of the kingdom is that the kingdom of God is an age of grace. The 'not yet' of the kingdom is that the kingdom of God is also an age of judgement.

Jesus' teaching on the kingdom of God

Since it formed the focal point of his manifesto, it is not surprising that Jesus had a lot to teach about the kingdom of God. Because it is such an intangible topic, it is again not surprising that a lot of what he had to say took the form of parables. How else could he teach about something like that? Interestingly, whenever Jesus talked about the kingdom of God in the form of a parable, he would say, 'The kingdom of God is like . . .'. The kingdom of God is like a mustard seed. The kingdom of God is like a man scattering seed on the ground and so on. Essentially, what Jesus is doing is saying that there is a sense in which we can know about the kingdom of God because it is related to ordinary life and everyday events. The *kairos*-quality of the kingdom can be experienced in and through the mundanity of *chronos*-objects and *chronos*-activities. However, he never says that, 'The kingdom of God is the same as . . .'. There is a real qualitative difference here. There is a mystery surrounding the nature of the kingdom of God even though that kingdom is identified with Jesus, the Word become flesh, and even though it can be likened to everyday events and objects.

But second, concerning Jesus' teaching on the kingdom, it is also important to recognize the inherent threat in what he was saying as far as the religious and political authorities were concerned. This should not surprise us because the power rested with them. They did not want this young upstart usurping their power and their position in society. Jesus was a very real political and social threat as symbolized by the overturning of the tables in the Temple.

The kingdom of God and the Spirit

Any consideration of the kingdom of God in Jesus' teaching and ministry must take into account the role of the Holy Spirit. The gift of the Spirit had, for many years, been considered a mark of the dawning of the new age. The gift of God's Spirit was an eagerly anticipated event within Judaism, dating back at least to the prophecy of Joel in 2.28–32: 'And it shall be after these things that I will pour out of my spirit on all flesh; your sons and your daughters shall prophesy, your old men shall dream dreams, and your young men shall see visions.' The coming of the Spirit of God would mark the dawning of the new age. In that context, we can revisit Luke 4 and see again the power of Jesus' words in the synagogue: 'The Spirit of the Lord is upon me because of which he has anointed me.' In the light of the expectations of Judaism that was one massive claim!

This, of course, was not lost on the other Gospel writers, either. Mark, for example, in 1.10 writes about Jesus' baptism: 'And immediately coming up from the water he saw the heavens open and the Spirit as a dove descending on to him.' Mark knew what he was saying when he wrote this! The coming of Jesus inaugurated the coming of the new age. The kingdom of God was present in Jesus and through him, and the Spirit of God upon him was the sign and seal of that. The stunning thing, of course, is that when Jesus taught about the kingdom of God between his resurrection and Ascension, he promised the same power of the Spirit to his disciples: 'But you will receive power, the Holy Spirit having come upon you, and you will be witnesses for me in both Jerusalem and in all Judea and Samaria and to the end of the earth' (Acts 1.8).

As we considered earlier, in the chapter on ascension, the community that Jesus inaugurated – the kingdom community – was also a community of the Spirit and continues to be so today. The kingdom of God continues to be present in the Church because we have been blessed with the power of the Holy Spirit. The role of the Holy Spirit in the kingdom of God is absolutely vital.

Youth ministry and kingdom discipleship

In *Jesus' Call to Discipleship*, James D. G. Dunn commented that,

> Mark sums up Jesus' call to discipleship in these words, 'The time is fulfilled, and the kingdom of God has come near; repent, and believe in the good news.' In these words are encapsulated the challenge and the attraction which Jesus evidently exerted on many of his contemporaries. (1992: 30)

There was a definite link between the kingdom of God and the call to discipleship in the teaching ministry of Jesus.

First, Jesus was clarifying for them the reality of God's rule. 'The time is fulfilled ... the kingdom of God has come near.' Jesus is consciously drawing a line under the Old Testament era and stressing the fact that the fulfilment of all those promises is now about to be made a reality in him. In the light of that, Jesus was calling his hearers to make an urgent decision: 'Repent and believe in the good news.' Here we see a twofold directive. *Repent*: turn around, head in a new direction. *Believe*: turn towards. Turn around and turn towards. That is the response of discipleship in the light of the kingdom of God breaking in. James Dunn said that the ministry of Jesus was 'An imminent crisis which demanded immediate response' (1992: 17). So what did the call of discipleship mean in Jesus' context? What were the hallmarks of his call to discipleship?

Crucially for youth ministry, we notice that the call to discipleship is good news to the marginalized. We touched on this a bit earlier but the truth is that the kingdom of God is an 'upside-down' kingdom with 'upside-down' ethical values. Those who are called into the kingdom are those on the margins of society. Discipleship is a call to the marginalized and the outcast. Let's just look briefly at four such examples.

First, the 12 disciples. The first community called by Jesus was the community of the 12 disciples. The fact that there were 12 is no co-incidence, of course. There had been 12 tribes of Israel and in calling 12 disciples, Jesus was making a symbolic point about the restoration of the 'true Israel'. But when we look at the 12 who were called it was not a community of the great and the good. It was a motley crew of fishermen and tax collectors and revolutionary soldiers; some of them weak, some of them strong. We must not forget, of course, that the Twelve were ministered to by a coterie of women which included in its ranks at least one reformed prostitute and who knows who else! The first Jesus community was an 'upside-down' community befitting an 'upside-down' kingdom.

Second, the imagery of sheep and the flock. In the Old Testament, the people of Israel had been referred to as the scattered sheep: 'He will feed his flock like a shepherd, he will gather the lambs in his arms' (Isaiah 40.11); 'And he shall stand and feed his flock in the strength of the Lord' (Micah 5.4) and so on. Just as the imagery of the 12 disciples picked up on the Old Testament idea of the 12 tribes, so Jesus picked up on the sheep and flock imagery to prove a point about his mission to restore the true Israel. 'I was sent only to the lost sheep of the house of Israel' (Matthew 15.24). 'Fear not, little flock, for it is your Father's good pleasure to give you the kingdom' (Luke 12.32) and so on.

Third, the image of the covenant. This is a key Old Testament image; the notion of the people of Israel living in a covenant relationship with God. Through this, Jesus goes right to the heart of Israel's relationship with God in the way he portrays his own sacrifice on the cross. At the Last Supper, Jesus says, 'Drink of it, all of you; for this is my blood of the covenant, which is poured out for many for the forgiveness of sins' (Matthew 26.28). The call to discipleship is the call to a renewed and restored covenant relationship with God.

Fourth, discipleship meant a sacrificial community-lifestyle. We have already considered Dietrich Bonhoeffer's famous maxim that, 'When Christ calls a man, he bids him come and die.' That, of course, merely echoes Jesus' own words that, 'If anyone would come after me, let him disown self and take up his cross and follow me. For whoever would save his life will lose it; and whoever loses his life for my sake will save it.' There is a cost to discipleship. We cannot just spiritualize this verse. There is a call on many to die for the gospel. There are many around the world today who are being martyred for the sake of Christ. Maybe the call will eventually be on us too.

We need to be sure of what it is we are saying when we call ourselves disciples of Jesus. We need to be sure what it is we are working towards when we try to lead young people into a relationship with Christ. We must be honest with them about the cost of discipleship as well as the benefits of salvation. But ultimately, the call to discipleship is good news for young people. God calls those on the margins of society, of whatever gender and with whatever life story, and promises an eternal covenantal relationship with them.

In conclusion

In conclusion, then, we note that the kingdom of God is an 'upside-down' kingdom. The ideas that hold the kingdom together are upside down. The ethical values of the kingdom are upside down. The constituency of people invited into the kingdom is upside down. My favourite verse in the Bible is Luke 3.1:

In the fifteenth year of the reign of Tiberius Caesar, Pontius Pilate being Governor of Judea, and Herod being tetrarch of Galilee, and his brother Philip tetrarch of the region of Ituraea and Trachonitis, and Lysanias being tetrarch of Abilene, during the high priesthood of Annas and Caiaphas, *the word of the Lord came upon John, son of Zechariah, in the desert.* [italics mine]

If God can choose John over and above all these titled people, there is hope for us all! That is the gospel message that a christological ministry must take to the young people living in a broken world. That is your task and mine.

Pause for thought

- What does the breaking in of the kingdom of God look like in the lives of your young people?
- Who are the young people on the margins of your community? What does the good news mean to them? How can you bring them that good news?
- What does discipleship mean to you? What do you teach young people to be the primary tenets of Christian discipleship?

and finally

- What changes will you need to make to your own ministry if you choose now to focus on *kairos* rather than *chronos*?

References

Athanasius, 1982. *On the Incarnation*. London and Oxford: Mowbray.

Barth, Karl, 1968 (1933). *The Epistle to the Romans*. Oxford and London: Oxford University Press.

Bornkamm, Günther, 1960. *Jesus of Nazareth*. London: Hodder and Stoughton.

Bosch, David, 1980. 'Salvation, Tomorrow *and* Today (A response to Adrio König).' *Theologia Evangelica* 13.2–3 (July–September 1980).

Brierley, Danny, 2003. *Joined Up*. Cumbria: Authentic.

Calvin, John, 1536. *Institutes of the Christian Religion*. Accessed through <www.ccel.org>.

Chrysostom, John, *Homilies on the First Epistle of St Paul to Timothy*. Homily XI. Accessed through <www.orthodoxchurchfathers.com>.

Claiborne, Shane, 2008. *Jesus for President: Politics for Ordinary Radicals*. Grand Rapids, MI: Zondervan.

Cox, Reginald Kennedy, 1931. *An Autobiography*. London: Hodder and Stoughton.

Cox, Reginald Kennedy, 1939. *Through the Dock Gates*. London: Michael Joseph.

Dunn, James D. G., 1992. *Jesus' Call to Discipleship*. Cambridge: Cambridge University Press.

Dyke, Henry Van, 'Gone from my Sight'. Accessed through <www.theribbon.com/poetry/gonefrommysight.asp>.

Farrow, Douglas, 1999. *Ascension and Ecclesia*. Edinburgh: T&T Clark.

Fee, Gordon, 2010. *Philippians*. Downers Grove, IL: InterVarsity Press.

Griffiths, Steve, 2003. *God of the Valley*. Oxford: Bible Reading Fellowship.

Griffiths, Steve, 2008. *A Christlike Ministry*. Haverhill, Essex: YTC Press.

Gutiérrez, Gustavo, 1973. *A Theology of Liberation: History, Politics and Salvation*. Maryknoll, NY: Orbis.

Hall, Douglas John, 2000. 'Confessing Christ in a Post-Christendom Context.' *The Ecumenical Review* 52.3: 410–17.

Irenaeus, 1989. *Against Heresies*. Ed. A. Roberts and J. Donaldson, *The Ante-Nicene Fathers, Volume I*. Edinburgh: T&T Clark.

Janzen, J. Gerald, 1985. *Job.* Atlanta, GA: John Knox.

Jeremias, Joachim, 1972. *New Testament Theology.* London: SCM Press.

Lash, Nicholas, 1984. *A Matter of Hope: A Theologian's Reflections on the Thought of Karl Marx.* Notre Dame, IN: University of Notre Dame Press.

Lewis, C. S., 1955. *Mere Christianity.* Glasgow: Collins.

Luther, Martin, 1520. *The Freedom of a Christian.* Accessed through <www.theologynetwork.org>.

Luther, Martin, 1526. *Against the Fanatics.* Cited by William C. Placher, 1988. *Readings in the History of Christian Theology, Volume 2.* Accessed through <books.google.co.uk>.

Lyotard, Jean-François, 1989. *The Lyotard Reader.* Oxford: Blackwell.

Moltmann, Jürgen, 1964. *Theology of Hope.* London: SCM Press.

Motyer, Alec, 1984. *The Message of Philippians.* Leicester: Inter-Varsity Press.

Moule, C. F. D., 1977. *The Origin of Christology.* Cambridge: Cambridge University Press.

Niebuhr, H. Richard, 1951. *Christ and Culture.* San Francisco, CA: HarperCollins.

Nouwen, Henri, 1979. *The Wounded Healer: Ministry in Contemporary Society.* London: Doubleday.

Packer, James, 1973. *Knowing God.* London: Hodder and Stoughton.

Passmore, Richard, 2003. *Meet Them Where They're At.* Bletchley, Milton Keynes: Scripture Union.

Prior, David, 1988. *Jesus and Power.* Leicester: Inter-Varsity Press.

Root, Andy, 2007. *Revisiting Relational Youth Ministry.* Downers Grove, IL: InterVarsity Press.

Runia, Klaas, 1995. *Crisis in Christology: Essays in Quest of Resolution.* Ed. W. R. Farmer; Livonia, MI: Dove.

Stott, John, 1990. *The Message of Acts.* Leicester: Inter-Varsity Press.

Stott, John, 1993. *The Contemporary Christian.* Leicester: Inter-Varsity Press.

Tillich, Paul, 1963. *The Eternal Now.* London: SCM Press.

Tillich, Paul, 1964 (1952). *The Courage to Be.* London and Glasgow: Collins.

Ward, Pete, 1997. *Youthwork and the Mission of God.* London: SPCK.

Warren, Rick, 1995. *The Purpose Driven Church.* Grand Rapids, MI: Zondervan.